Rural Development: Research Priorities

North Central Regional Center for Rural Development

Rural Development:
Research Priorities

HN
90
·C6
R77

The Iowa State University Press / **Ames** / 1973

A collection of papers presented during a symposium (Developing Research Priorities on the Problems of Rural Development) at Zion, Illinois, May 9–11, 1972; sponsored by the North Central Regional Center for Rural Development, the North Central Regional Research Strategy Committee on Rural Community and Resource Development, and the Farm Foundation.

Volume Editor: **Larry R. Whiting**

© 1973 The Iowa State University Press
Ames, Iowa 50010. All rights reserved

Composed and printed by
The Iowa State University Press

First edition, 1973

Library of Congress Cataloging in Publication Data

Main entry under title:

Rural development: research priorities.

"A collection of papers presented during a symposium (Developing research priorities on the problems of rural development) Zion, Illinois, May 9–11, 1972; sponsored by the North Central Regional Center for Rural Development, the North Central Regional Research Strategy Committee on Rural Community and Resource Development, and the Farm Foundation."

1. Community development—Research—United States—Congresses.   I. North Central Regional Center for Rural Development.   II. North Central Regional Center for Rural Development. North Central Regional Research Strategy Committee on Rural Community and Resource Development.   III. Farm Foundation, Chicago.

HN90.C6R77   309.2′63′0973   73–13548
ISBN 0–8138–1450–2

CONTENTS

FOREWORD

RURAL COMMUNITY development involves a vast set of phenomena and relationships ranging over problems of health and recreational services in rural areas, rural industrialization and job creation in smaller towns, guidance for workers displaced from increasingly large and technologically advanced farms, methods of financing local and state governments to provide equitable distribution of services and their costs, railroad abandonment and transportation systems for elderly people as well as for farm commodities, regional economic development, goals for and measurement of the quality of life in farm-oriented communities, and a host of others.

Currently no land-grant university in the North Central Region has a research program adequate for the problems of rural communities in its state. Both funds and capable research personnel are extremely scarce relative to the number and intensity of problems. Hence priorities in rural community development are extremely important. The pressure of time and paucity of funds (for example under the Rural Development Act of 1972) have caused federal and state research administrators to suggest that projects should be selected which will show "quick results." Speedy results are most likely to be shown if projects concentrate on towns and cities that have already established momentum in rural industrialization and auxiliary activities. With some research aid and ample communication machinery, tangible results can be shown quickly in the form of increased plant investment, community income, and employment.

But even with these results generated in a short time span, is this the most important set of problems in the state? Certainly rural industrialization is an important component of any state program in community development, but further industrialization of communities that already have something going may not represent the most intense problems of rural communities. Other problems which cannot readily show results may be equally or more intense. If concentration because of the pressures of time and research budgets were on further advancement of communities in an upswing of development, we might simply bring more gains to those already realizing them while burdening communities in the process of decline with further deterioration in population, employment, and capital values.

vii

The vast problem complex of rural development is one of equity in the distribution of the benefits and costs of our ongoing and rapid national economic growth and technological progress. At the farm level both public and private funds have gone into new technologies which have been successfully applied on farms of growing size and productivity. These technologies have brought gains in the form of higher income and asset values to farm operators with the capital necessary to put them to use and remain in business. But they have been costly to older farmers who can no longer compete, to workers displaced from farms, and especially to small-town merchants and service workers whose economic opportunities have dwindled with the farm population. At the national level we have pursued economic growth as a means of averting unemployment and recessions of the magnitude experienced in the 1930s and earlier. But in pursuing growth as a single-valued national goal, we have paid little attention to the geographic or spatial distribution of it. Consequently, most of it has gone to urban centers. Rural areas are further drained of economic opportunity and thus have a greater burden or cost fall upon them. As a nation we did not get concerned with distribution of the benefits and costs of national economic development until growing burdens of social unrest and environmental degradation fell heavily upon the central city.

Obviously the distribution of costs and benefits of technological change and national economic growth is the core of the rural development problem. How do we bring gains to the commercial farm sector without imposing mammoth sacrifices on the rural town and service sectors about them? How do we maintain or create relevant employment opportunities and a favorable living environment in rural areas comparable to those generated through national goals and public investments for the cities and their suburbs?

The selection of research projects that can show results in a year and a half clearly excludes the majority of rural community problems. The task of creating equitable tax assessment and fiscal systems cannot be accomplished in that period of time. Neither can solutions to the problems of communities lacking opportunities in development or of creating efficient rural health delivery systems. Thus rural development research programs must have priorities based on criteria other than what can show the most in the shortest time. Such criteria would nearly always lead us from solving the complex problems of communities and population strata that now bear the major burden of sacrifice from ongoing farm technological advance and national economic growth concentrated at urban centers.

What are the criteria upon which research and educational priorities can be based when the problem set is large and the resources are few? The chapters in this book are directed toward this and related questions. The land-grant universities of the region, through their agricultural experiment stations, have large public funds devoted to research. Questions are posed of whether these institutions have made only meager reallocations of their efforts, leaving the major concentration of research to remain on technologies that encourage even fewer and larger farm units and intensify the decline of employment and economic activity in the surrounding community. Questions also are posed of whether research projects bearing the label of rural development are sometimes only conventional projects relabeled to qualify for funds earmarked for more central rural community development problems.

These are important and serious questions which surround the formation of effective rural development research programs. They are, however, the most important social, economic, and administrative questions in the North Central Region. The implementation of effective priorities and research programs consistent with deepening rural community problems must rest with the administrators who manage research programs and the scientists who perform the actual research function.

EARL O. HEADY
*Director, North Central
Regional Center for
Rural Development*

PREFACE

WE ARE at a stage of development today where the engineer and the planner are on a collision course with the economist and sociologist. After the crash the future course of these sciences will be a median and compromise between the angles of approach. Relating this concept to the present "state of the art," we are approaching the point of impact that will allow our universities, with their diverse citizenry, to capture the imagination of Congress in focusing on people's problems. Through this systems approach—brought about by stimulating the imagination and engaging the obvious and latent expertise inherent in the system—we and our colleagues in engineering, medicine, education, law, home economics, the sciences, and humanities as a community of scholars should be able to kindle the light of innovation. So illuminated, the wisdom of those who forged the organic act will provide the incentive to underscore relevance and through the guise of state's rights, fashion new funding mechanisms to permit the true coalition of the sciences.

The time has come when a parallel with the experiment stations can constitute the core of a new opportunity that will allow the university to apply its competencies to the solution of the problems of the rural communities and their people.

We have reached the point in time when we must return to the cradles of this new thrust—this new concept that calls for a different aggregation of science disciplines. The challenge is not to conceptualize a model but to move out with visionary programs that will capture the imaginations of our colleagues and gain the confidence of the public as these programs begin to solve the relevant problems of rural people. The challenge is to provide visibility, to set into motion a new thrust—a conglomerate of disciplines motivated to be of service to our rural communities and their people.

J. P. MAHLSTEDE
Associate Director, Iowa Agriculture and Home Economics Experiment Station, Ames

Rural Development: Research Priorities

NATIONAL OUTLOOK AND PERSPECTIVE

ORVILLE G. BENTLEY

RURAL DEVELOPMENT has a new face. The concept has matured since True D. Morse advanced the idea into a national program in the mid-1950s. There are growing indications that the rural development concept is reaching a "take-off point," that we may be moving into a new stage of development for rural America. The challenge is to find an avenue for bringing solutions to problems that have been so painstakingly identified and cataloged over twenty years of experience.

While it is impossible to document the broad scope of literature that has been published on the subject, some significant statements present a consensus of concern on the problems of rural people and the plight of rural America. The President's National Advisory Commission on Rural Poverty, established by President Johnson, reported its findings in "The People Left Behind." This report pointed to the poverty, poor housing, and comparative lack of social and economic development in rural America. Another report (1970) from the task force on rural development created by President Nixon is summarized in "A New Life for the Country." A plethora of rural development legislation has been introduced in Congress, much of which has been passed in laws that deal with migratory labor, housing in rural areas, special programs for providing credit, and other federally supported programs aimed at assisting rural people to improve their economic well-being and quality of living. Other legislation provides for a much expanded program of research and extension to be carried out through our nation's system of land-grant universities. To these governmental reports on rural America one should add the many

ORVILLE G. BENTLEY is Dean of Agriculture, University of Illinois, Urbana.

significant publications prepared under the aegis of such organizations as the Iowa State University Center for Agricultural and Rural Development, the Agricultural Policy Institute of North Carolina State University, and the Farm Foundation whose concern for rural America had its origins in the minds of its founders in 1933.

While it is difficult to suggest that a single statement might summarize the views that flow through many of these reports, perhaps no one statement better accomplishes this goal than one from "A New Life for the Country": "The purpose of rural development is to create job opportunities, community service, better quality of living, and an improved social and physical environment for the small cities, villages, and farm communities in rural America."

RESEARCH AND EDUCATIONAL FRAMEWORK. Through at least two decades of experience, research and educational approaches to a concept of rural development have matured to the point that specific goals can be set forth for programs in these areas. The importance of the concept to our national health has been widely recognized, and the relevance of developing an educational base is being increasingly stressed by politicians, educators, and local opinion leaders. Having reached the present state of maturity about the unique problems of rural America, the time is propitious to begin an intensified effort for (1) setting forth viable research and educational program alternatives and (2) evolving an educational framework for implementing these programs. The nation's land-grant universities have expertise in research and an operational concept for extension education that has served agriculture effectively for several decades. The agricultural experiment stations and the extension services have an administrative structure capable of coming to grips with an interdisciplinary, problem-oriented effort in research and extension programs in rural development. Besides an understanding of the nuances of internal relationships of rural communities, staff members in land-grant colleges have a sensitivity for intricacies within the forces variously described as the rural-urban interphase, the agricultural industry's marketing and processing infrastructure, and interregional and even international dimensions of agriculture.

The Senate's version of the Rural Development Act of 1972 stresses that research and educational programs in rural development should be centered in land-grant universities. Those institutions must take up the challenge to initiate new research programs designed to provide a factual basis for improved decision making. The approaches to research and extension education programs must be made on an interdisciplinary basis, recognizing that new alignments may be required within land-grant universities to provide the expertise for the broad coverage of problems to be researched and for which new educational programs may need to be devised.

It is also imperative that the regional organizations representing the agricultural experiment stations and the cooperative extension services place at the top of their agendas of concerns the matter of organizing a structure that will reflect the regional and national aspects of rural development extension and research programs. A strong regional approach to planning research has strengthened the ability of participating teams and individual scientists to contribute information to the solution of regional and national problems. Interregional coordination of research by individual units must be sought if we are to deal with problems of the magnitude inherent in rural development education and research.

INVOLVING PEOPLE. The success of a program can be greatly influenced by the process used to identify the developmental targets or goals; the people concerned must be involved! One of the "hang-ups" in rural development has been the difficulty in reaching a consensus on goals acceptable to the different groups of people having a legitimate and vested interest in its future directions. An approach directed entirely to the needs of the agricultural sector falls short of meeting the real needs of many rural nonfarm residents in the small towns and cities facing problems created by the changing patterns of rural living; a program that fails to recognize agriculture as the predominant industry of the rural areas is doomed to failure. One of the cardinal rules for success in agricultural research has been an understanding of the "territory" and the ability of agricultural scientists to identify with the problems and needs of the agricultural enterprise. This concept must not be forgotten in planning rural development research. In years gone by, the progress and development of rural areas has been greatest—even dramatic—when we have established a consensus for a given developmental goal. Such cooperative joint ventures as rural electrification, creation of the farm credit system, the National Association of Soil Conservation Districts that were developed in support of soil and water conservation efforts, and the general cooperative movement to provide services to rural residents are examples.

A realistic cataloging of the current assets and liabilities of rural America is needed to provide bench marks for many purposes—setting research priorities and evaluating progress (or lack of it) in such areas as housing, job opportunities, governmental structures, health services, and educational opportunities. Research and rural development must be aware of parallel developments occurring in the revitalization of metropolitan areas. Without minimizing the role of government and the influx of resources from metropolitan areas into rural areas, growth, if it is to occur in rural areas, must get healthy and vigorous support from the people living there now. External investment and leadership can help, but the resources, people, and other ingredients for growth must be homegrown.

While many of these "values" are subjective and intangible (as is often the preference to living in a crowded urban center), people build in preferences for rural living. For those rural people (and perhaps nonrural people as well) holding these views about life in the country, the rural environment and "way of life" are seen as social and cultural advantages with economic implications. The question is How much do the real and perceived benefits of rural living offset the disparity in service availability vis-à-vis an urban area? Poverty is poverty, whether in rural or urban areas, but not all the people in rural areas are poor. The same comment applies to the adequacy and quality of health and educational opportunities. A key to success in rural development will be the degree to which programs can be made to appeal to a widely accepted belief on how rural America can be made better, recognizing the heterogeneity of the rural people and the social and economic values they hold to be important to *them*. However, increased emphasis on the quality of life and preservation of our environment and on establishing greater economic and social equality for all people will have an important bearing on the desire of rural residents to make changes or, conversely, to maintain the status quo. Rural development must have an appeal not only to farmers, ranchers, and nonfarm residents but to the city dweller who wishes to preserve his "unseen" property rights to open space and the recreational opportunities he finds in the countryside.

PUBLIC AND PRIVATE COOPERATION. The identification of action-oriented agencies of government with the capacity to serve rural people is in itself a research task. Rural people are increasingly concerned in the overlapping of agencies that provide services required by them. The complexity of jurisdictions dealing with rural America suggests that perhaps some new administrative arrangement, new organization, and new levels of cooperation between the public and private sectors may be one of the first orders of business in rural development research. Coupled with reexamining the role of government agencies is the need to review the role of organizations created by rural people themselves—farm organizations and cooperatives—in an effort to orient their activities to serve the needs of a modern rural society. Can the action-oriented government agencies, private organizations, and universities work jointly in an effort not only to identify research needs and opportunities for educational programs but to identify parts of the problem? Such cooperation would enable the agencies having a legitimate interest in development in rural areas to take responsibility for handling an appropriate part of the larger problems. In reaching decisions on the division of the problem, it is important that the planning be done in a way that the various activities result in findings that might be additive. Comparability and the need to keep planning on individual efforts as a part of the whole are of utmost importance.

Social equity must be a pervasive thread in rural development; hence the implications of social justice must be considered in research on all problems.

Research in demography in rural areas has been given a great deal of attention. Research on population distribution and the nature of the rural population is an important bench mark. This research must be continued and attention given to plans for an adequate census program to provide research workers with accurate, reliable data on salient features of the rural population.

Rural and urban social institutions will become increasingly similar as people seek to utilize all of the socioeconomic tools available to the nation as a whole. Educational challenges in a rural development program will be to help people who have moved from urban areas understand a rural-based community and to help rural people understand the values brought to their communities by people from urban areas.

The final item is the attitudes and policies that should be uppermost in the minds of the research workers and that should be given cognizance by administrators as they gear up for a broadened program. Rural development research should be done by people sensitive to the workings and interrelationships important to a dynamic agricultural economy. This new effort will likely be best served by a new version of the agricultural research worker and the land-grant university. Many of the same techniques and approaches will suffice, but there must be a recognition of the broad scope of rural development problems. Perhaps the missing link, if we look ahead to rural development, is the lack of a development model that brings together the multiplicity of factors essential to a successful developmental approach. The model must identify the problem elements, but it also must consider the matter of resource allocation. How many resources will be needed to initiate a successful research program? How can these resources be obtained? How much can be obtained by the reallocation of funds already available to the experiment station director or to the director of the cooperative extension programs in the several states? Can reasonably new funding be tapped? Will the agricultural experiment station have access to the funds that are administered through the Environmental Protection Agency; Health, Education and Welfare; the U.S. Public Health Service; and the U.S. Department of Commerce? These agencies have many more funds for potential rural development programs than the USDA. Consequently, the agricultural experiment station has to serve an integrating role if it is to draw these funds to assist in research or development programs for rural areas.

INTERDISCIPLINARY RESEARCH. The success of the rural development research enterprise will depend on the ability of the coordinator to bring together a critical group of experts, university and nonuniversity, that will function as an interdisciplinary task force with sufficient capability to cope with the multiplicity of problems found in rural America. Parochialism, where it still exists within the agricultural research enterprise, must give way to broader approaches commensurate with the scope and complexity of the problem. Greater attention must be given to methodology and plans that will produce new approaches to mobilize the resources of interdisciplinary teams or research task forces established within the land-grant university. The final chapters of "A New Life for the Country" lists the research areas vital to the development of a comprehensive program of rural development.

The challenge to the land-grant universities is clear; they have an opportunity to be the fountain of knowledge in yet another area of societal concern—rural America. Campus leadership should come from the College of Agriculture whose members have experience in working with rural people and have been involved in joint cooperative research and educational programs with the federal and state agencies. The basic approach in agricultural research and extension education is interdisciplinary; thus there is an academic and intellectual link to other campus departments for the exchange of ideas and knowledge. Involvement in the rural development concept, if properly done, will be in the public interest (rural and urban) and thus will further the spirit of J. B. Turner's dream for a "public university" that would direct its scholarly and scientific endeavors to solving the problems of rural people.

CHAPTER TWO

SCOPE AND NATIONAL CONCERNS

JERRY B. WATERS

TODAY'S RURAL DEVELOP-
MENT is new because the term
"rural" does not mean rural in the old sense of farm and village. Its
meaning has been escalated. Beginning in the Johnson administration and continuing in the Nixon administration, "rural," for administrative purposes, is equated with nonmetropolitan America—
that is, everything outside the cities of 50,000 and the immediate surrounding high-density territory (100 or more persons per square mile).
With certain exceptions, this is everything outside the Standard Metropolitan Statistical Areas. This definition encompasses most of the
country's geography and about 30 percent of its people.

Today's rural development is new because it is no longer synonymous with poverty and depressed areas. The Rural Development Act
of 1972 defines areas of eligibility by population numbers, not by the
numbers of dollars earned by that population. This is one reason the
current rural development movement should not be seen as simply an
extension of the old Rural Area Development program, the Economic
Development Administration, and the Appalachian Regional Commission. This is not to say that the current rural development is un-
concerned with poverty but rather that it is concerned with much
more.

Today's rural development is new because its objective is improved conditions in all of rural America so that more people will
have the opportunity to remain there. Thus it differs from some of
the older efforts which seemed to be aimed more toward preparing
people to leave rural areas.

Today's rural development is new in the sense that it challenges

JERRY B. WATERS is Administrative Assistant to Senator James Pearson
of Kansas.

the concept that massive urbanization is somehow dictated by iron-clad laws of economics that cannot and should not be tampered with.

THE NATIONAL DIALOGUE. How did this view of rural development come into being? How did the current rural development
movement get started? What forces triggered this outpouring of
preachments from Washington politicians about the desirability and
indeed the necessity of a national commitment to rural development?

In a certain sense, the current rural development movement had
its beginnings in the fires of Watts in August 1965. The early efforts
to explain Watts emphasized that the rioters were primarily newly
arrived southern migrants demoralized and eventually terrorized by
this new urban environment. No matter that later studies revealed
that most of the rioters were older residents; a spark had been ignited,
and for the first time since the 1930s the country began to take a
serious look at the question of rural-to-urban migration. Calvin Beale
of the USDA came up with the revealing statistic that requests to the
Population Studies Group for rural-to-urban migration data increased
250 percent between 1964 and 1968.[1]

During this same period—partly because of Watts and the three
long hot summers that followed, partly because of New York City's
widely heralded "slide toward chaos,"[2] partly because of electrical
brownouts, and partly because of a crystalization of our awareness of
the seriousness of urban pollution—the nation was forced to take a
new hard look at the conditions of the cities. In this reexamination
we came to realize that the problems were much worse and a great
deal more pervasive than we had earlier believed and that the problems extended far beyond the black ghettos.

We had known for a number of years that our cities were in
trouble, and we had responded perhaps half-heartedly with the infu-
sion of billions of dollars for housing, water and sewers, and urban
renewal. But after this very considerable effort the cities were worse
off than ever before. Their air was increasingly polluted, the sources
of their water supplies contaminated, their traffic all the more snarled,
their crime rates higher, their welfare rolls ever larger. And virtually
every big city mayor was proclaiming his city on the verge of bank-
ruptcy.

In the fall and winter of 1966 Senator Abraham Ribicoff, Senator
Edward Kennedy, and Senator Jacob Javits conducted an extensive
and unusually highly publicized set of hearings on the problems of

1. "Rural Changes in the 1960's," *46th National Agricultural Outlook Conference*, Washington, D.C., Feb. 18, 1969.
2. During the period 1966–69, New York City was hit with three teachers'
strikes, a garbagemen's strike, a police "sick-in," a firemen's slowdown, and
a host of other problems which prompted Mayor John Lindsay to proclaim,
"The question now is whether we can continue to survive as a city."

the cities. The most significant feature of that long recital of urban woes was the suggestion that if we were really serious about solving the urban problem, the price tag would be an additional trillion dollars over the next ten years.[3]

This may have been a reasonably accurate projection of what was needed, but there was no stampede to increase taxes and raise the federal budget accordingly—partly because there was no agreement on how the money should be spent even if sums of that magnitude were available but also because of a growing sense that money alone would not cure the urban sickness. Thus, during the last half of the 1960s, the "crises of the cities" became a commonplace term in the national dialogue. Many a journalist and politician asked, only half rhetorically, Can our cities survive?

Out of this massive public soul-searching, a new notion began to take hold—quite possibly one of the most significant new ideas of the post–World War II period. There was a dawning recognition that the gigantic problems of the cities were an inevitable result of helter-skelter urbanization. This was more than a realization that we had failed miserably to plan our cities properly; it was a recognition that a great imbalance was developing in the spatial distribution of our people—a growing belief that many of our social, economic, and political ills were the result of our big cities being too big.

Secretary of Agriculture Orville Freeman, who had been urging a policy of rural-urban balance for several years, now found an audience. Papers like the *Washington Post,* which had long since forgotten there was a rural America, began to praise the Secretary for his vision.

A number of congressmen began to propose that the economic development of our rural areas was one of the best ways to ease the burdens of the cities. Senator James Pearson, introducing his Rural Job Development Act of 1967, put it this way:

> In our efforts to deal with crises of the cities we have come to realize that the challenge is not simply to make them more efficient and livable for more and more people but how to keep more and more people from crowding into them. For we are beginning to recognize that the cause of many of the problems which now plague our cities can be traced to the overcrowding of people and excessive concentration of industry.

Beginning in 1966 and continuing through to the present, an increasing number of Senate and House members have called for programs of rural development in order to slow the tide of migrants to the already overcrowded and overburdened cities. And outside the Congress we have seen an impressive number of endorsements of the concept that we ought to try to curb rural outmigration.

President Johnson's National Advisory Commission on Civil Dis-

---

3. This would be about $100 billion per year. At that time it was estimated that we were spending about $28 billion per year.

orders pointed to the need to slow the tide of the rural poor to the urban ghettos. His Commission on Rural Poverty indicated that the ghettos could never be substantially improved if the rural poor kept moving into them. In 1968 the Advisory Commission on Intergovernmental Relations issued a solid plea for rural-urban balance.

The 1968 National Governors Conference declared in somewhat exaggerated language that "population imbalance is at the core of nearly every major social problem facing our nation today." The governors called on Congress to adopt a policy of balanced national growth, a position they have adopted in each successive conference. In 1969 the U.S. Conference of Mayors called for more aid to small communities so they could absorb more of the projected population increase.

In 1970 President Nixon's Task Force on Rural Development painted a dark picture of our cities beset with "pollution, transportation paralysis, housing blight, and crime" and argued that further rural migration to the cities would necessarily compound these problems. The report of the White House National Goals Research Staff gave prominent attention to the need to devise means to divert population pressure from the great cities. In his 1970 State of the Union message, President Nixon declared, "We must create a new rural environment that will not only stem the migration to urban centers but reverse it."

Thus the original impetus to today's rural development came from a growing sense of concern and frustration over the crises of the cities rather than from an aroused awareness of the plight of rural areas.

Therefore, rural development may be defined as a shorthand term for efforts aimed at improving economic and social conditions in rural communities, both poor and underdeveloped, which in current usage means most of nonmetropolitan America. These improvements are sought for reasons of equity—that is, to erase the rural deficit in such areas as income, housing, and health care—and as a means of discouraging rural-to-urban migration and eventually reversing it to some unspecified extent.

The distinguishing characteristic of today's rural development is the drive to redirect population and economic growth patterns. It aims to encourage the dispersal of people and industry rather than their concentration. It is driven by the belief that the uncontrolled gathering of people and industry into the sprawling metropolitan agglomerations is undesirable because those areas—particularly the very large ones—are seen as increasingly economically inefficient, socially destructive, and politically unmanageable. It is reinforced by the old and still powerful strain in American thought that the small community is sociologically preferable to the large city.

The term rural development itself may not survive, but the concern for the development of the small community is rather solidly entrenched for several reasons.

1. We now know that the urbanization process must be brought under some control and that retaining and increasing population in nonmetropolitan areas will be a positive factor in this effort. The very fact that the current rural development movement arose in very considerable part out of the crises of the cities gives it an important additional source of strength.

2. We have developed a more heightened awareness of the extent to which rural areas do lag in many of the socioeconomic indicators, so considerations of equity will continue to be a strong driving force.

3. Rural development has a fairly strong ideological or value underpinning. America was born on the farm and in the small village, and although it has long since moved to the city, we have always had some doubts as to whether the move was wise. We have always had a love-hate relationship with our cities. We have accepted the classic Greek view of the city as the seat of civilization and the modern Western view of the city as the center of economic power, but we have also wondered whether or not Rome did in fact fall because it became too "citified." We never fully embraced Jefferson's pronouncement of the cities as "cancers on the body politic," but we have never forgotten it. At the same time we have always had a special affinity for the small town and farm community. We may have criticized it for being narrow and provincial, but we have never feared it. Indeed, rural America has generally been looked to as a source of stabilizing strength and the repository of many important social virtues.

4. Politicians have found that advocacy of rural development provides an excellent vehicle for communicating with their small-town constituents and that support for rural development is politically popular.

Because rural development is a legitimate part of the general recognition that we should be trying to impose some semblance of spatial balance to our growing population, rural development proposals are often supported by urban interests. Nevertheless, in terms of initiating proposals and guiding them through the public policy-making process, the burden falls primarily on rural political representatives.

An increasing number of congressmen are willing to perform this task, and they have done reasonably well. However, one of the things lacking is an organized rural lobby that can generate legislative ideas and marshal political muscle for their enactment. The farm organizations are divided by commodities and philosophy and are rather suspicious of the whole rural development thing in the first place. There is no organization that effectively ties farm and town together and is capable of articulating their concerns and mobilizing their political strength. At present, the National Rural Electric Cooperative Association is the most effective general rural lobby, but it is limited in many respects.

In 1971 the Coalition for Rural America was organized to fill the gap. If it survives and becomes a viable political lobby, the cause of rural development will be considerably enhanced.

Despite the soaring rhetoric of many of its advocates, improving of the condition of rural America will not cure all the ills of urban America, although it will surely help. Neither will the development of our rural communities result in a pattern of fully balanced national growth, although again it will surely help. To keep our sense of perspective, we must recognize that the population balance has already tilted too far toward the metropolitan side; it can be brought back only partially.

Between 1960 and 1970, 74 percent of the growth in metropolitan areas was natural—that is, due to an excess of births over deaths. Of the 26 percent increase due to inmigration a considerable portion was because of foreign immigration. Thus even if all rural migration were to be brought to a halt, the metropolitan areas would continue to grow at a striking rate. Therefore, balanced national growth is much bigger and much more comprehensive than evening out the growth rates between nonmetropolitan and metropolitan areas. Most of the "balancing" is going to have to be done within metropolitan America. Some people tend to treat rural development and balanced national growth as synonymous. Rural development is a part of balanced national growth, but it is not the whole of it.

Not long after the 1970 State of the Union message in which President Nixon urged a reversal of the migration trends, a subcommittee of the President's Domestic Council was assigned the task of putting together a comprehensive rural development and balanced national growth policy to be proposed in his 1971 State of the Union message. The Cabinet secretaries and their staffs met regularly throughout late summer and fall. The assignment was treated with utmost seriousness and undertaken with high expectation, but in the end the effort failed. No comprehensive policy was produced, and the administration fell back to the policy position of rural revenue sharing, government reorganization, welfare reform, and the strengthening of existing programs having an impact on rural development.

This rather massive effort on the part of the Domestic Council failed to achieve its goal largely because the goal was realistically beyond their reach at that particular time. The effort got under way originally because the Nixon administration was being urged by a number of congressmen and other political supporters to do something in the area of rural development, and the President was sympathetic. But rather than restricting the effort of producing a coordinated set of policy recommendations to "create a new rural environment" which the President had urged in his 1970 State of the Union message, the council took up the task of trying to develop a truly comprehensive, broad policy for balanced national growth. Why treat just part of the problem? Why not go after the whole thing?

But the whole thing was impossible to get hold of. First of all, the technical information base was not there. Comprehensive data and economic and sociological models needed to evaluate alternative policies were lacking. Secondly, there had not been enough national political dialogue, and there was little clear understanding of what was politically acceptable and what was not. How would the big city mayors react? What would the governors do? What would Congress accept? In short, the informational and political frameworks necessary for the formation of broad, precedent-setting national policy were not well enough defined. Major shifts in national policy must undergo an evolutionary process for both technical and political reasons.

Certainly we should continue to move toward the development of a comprehensive policy of national growth, but the search for a national growth policy should not be allowed to become a barrier to rural development. We are at that stage in the evolutionary process where we can do some concrete and worthwhile things to improve economic and social conditions in rural America; we should proceed to do them and not be deterred by the argument that we should not move ahead with programs for rural community development until we know all there is to know about national growth and how to control it so as to achieve the goals that we can all agree upon.

We recognize the hazards of taking public policy action without adequate knowledge of the consequences. But certainly no great harm will have been done if we are able to encourage the creation of more new job-creating industries in rural areas; to erase the rural deficit in such areas as income, education, and health care; to improve social and cultural opportunities in our farm communities. If we are successful in doing these things, we will very likely have slowed the rural-to-urban migration and therefore taken a significant step toward balanced national growth.

LEGISLATIVE RECORD. One of the first clearly identifiable pieces of legislation was the addition of a rural development title to the Agriculture Act of 1970, which stated:

> The Congress commits itself to a sound balance between rural and urban America. The Congress considers this balance so essential to the

peace, prosperity and welfare of all our citizens that the highest priority must be given to the revitalization and development of rural areas.

The title created no programs but did lay down a set of reporting requirements on the executive branch.

The Rural Development Act of 1972 is the first direct follow-through to the rural development commitment written into the 1970 act. As passed by the Senate, the act would move the Farmers Home Administration into the business of rural economic development in a fairly major way by authorizing it to make several types of loans for commercial and industrial purposes as well as for community facilities. The agency would be divided into a Farm Development Administration and a Rural Enterprise and Community Development Administration.

Other titles would strengthen water and soil conservation programs, particularly to provide special assistance to projects that will help link conservation efforts and rural community development programs. Of particular interest to this group is Title VI, "Rural Development and Small Farm Research and Education," which directs the Secretary of Agriculture to establish a program of rural development and small farm research to be carried out primarily through the land-grant universities and the cooperative extension service. The authorization is $50 million for fiscal 1974 with increases to $135 million by fiscal 1976. The act also has a $500 million general rural revenue sharing provision.

One piece of legislative action which has largely been overlooked is the provision written into the Federal-Aid Highway Act of 1970 setting up a program of demonstration projects intended to illustrate the role of highways in small community development. Future expansion of this program might well be of major significance.

The fiscal 1971 budget provided a $3 million appropriation for rural development research to be administered through the agricultural experiment stations.

This rather meager legislative list does not tell the whole story, however. Other actions can be attributed at least in part to the heightened interest in rural development.

The funding level for the Farmers Home Administration housing and water and sewer programs is substantially higher than otherwise would be the case. For example, assistance for housing has more than tripled since 1969. This is due in considerable part to the support of the Nixon administration.

The Congress has expanded the Resource Conservation and Development district program, largely because of the growing interest in rural development. Interest in rural development has also served to produce an effective counter to the pressures (primarily from the Office of Management and Budget) to curtail certain conservation programs and the REA loan program. The Housing and Urban Development Act of 1968 contains stronger provisions for rural housing and nonmetropolitan planning partly because of the rural development movement; grants for nonmetropolitan planning districts have tripled since 1969.

Housing and Urban Development has recently funded a $400,000 experimental project in rural Connecticut using communication technology in an effort to lure people from congested cities to rural areas. This is an outgrowth of a study by the National Academy of Engineering for Housing and Urban Development, which concluded that "many of the cities' problems are caused by high density living conditions" and that communication technology can be used to counter the trend toward urban compaction.[4]

During 1971 alone over 130 distinctively rural development bills were introduced in the House and Senate. The major proposals are those which would establish a new credit structure to help finance rural community development and a tax incentive program to encourage industry to locate in rural areas.

The Federal Rural Development Credit Agency, originally proposed by Senator Hubert Humphrey and Senator Herman Talmadge and made a part of the Rural Development Act of 1972, was voted down on the Senate floor. Senator Pearson's proposal to provide special tax incentives for new job-creating industries in rural areas was adopted by the Senate as an amendment to the Revenue Act of 1971 but was dropped in the conference committee. Other proposals would strengthen rural health care, establish an emergency rural housing program, strengthen rural water and sewer assistance, improve air service to small communities, and establish a national rural development research center.

ROLE OF THE LAND-GRANT SYSTEM. The establishment of the land-grant system, and later the creation of its sister institutions the extension service and the experiment station, was one of the most important pieces of social legislation in the 19th century. Together these three institutions came to constitute the finest vehicle for community service, adult education, technology creation, and technology transfer in the Western world.

One measure of the success of this institutional triad is the tremendous productivity of American agriculture. There have been other sources and other reasons for this surge in the productive efficiency of American agriculture, but this triad has been a major force

4. National Academy of Engineering Committee on Telecommunication, "Communication Technology for Urban Improvement," Report to the Department of Housing and Urban Development, Contract No. H-1221, June 1971, p. 405.

in the technological revolution in agriculture—a revolution that has depopulated the countryside and eroded the economic base of thousands of our small towns and cities. Thus the land-grant system has had an enormous impact on shaping our present population distribution patterns. It did not set out to do this, but this is the end result.

The land-grant system has too long ignored the social consequences of its technological contribution. It has been too slow in recognizing its responsibility to the larger rural community. This is not to say that agriculture should be ignored; indeed there should be renewed attention to the needs of the small family farm. But the need for emphasis on agricultural production technology has diminished, and the needs of the greater rural community must now be considered.

In most states there is no other institutional arrangement that has the potential for servicing the needs and aspirations of small communities. This institutional triad can make an enormous contribution in analyzing community and area resources and economic growth potentials and in meeting the needs of small communities for technical assistance and planning and transfer of technology.

The time is propitious for a refocusing and redefinition of the goals of the land-grant system; indeed, the current rural development movement demands it. Changes have been under way in many states for several years, but the progress to date looks small when measured against the potential. The effort to realign can be difficult and time-consuming, and this expanded role of community service cannot be achieved simply by a readjustment of internal priorities. Additional financial support will be needed.

Despite the financial squeeze on most states, their legislatures can probably be persuaded to increase appropriations if they are convinced that the land-grant system can execute a set of worthwhile community service programs. Also the prospects for increased federal aid are good. Congress did not approve funds for the regional centers for rural development in 1970, and only $3 million annually has been earmarked for the experiment station-sponsored rural development research, but this situation is explained largely by the fact that there has been very little organized constituency effort to support these proposals. Most senators and congressmen who endorse rural development are only dimly aware of the role that the land-grant system might play in this effort if properly funded.

On the other hand, Title VI of the Rural Development Act of 1972 is a good example of what can be done when Congress is presented with a workable proposal by the land-grant people. This proposal was initiated by Chancellor D. B. Varner of the University of Nebraska at one of the field hearings of the Subcommittee on Rural Development and later perfected by one of the association committees. The Senate Agricultural Committee was convinced, and the rest of the Senate readily accepted it.

One of the priorities in rural development should be a research project on how the land-grant system can better convince the Congress of the role it is capable of playing in the rural development effort. The growing interest in rural development presents the land-grant system with a great opportunity to broaden its horizon and redesign its community service programs. Given the right leadership and the right breaks, the land-grant system can once again be one of the great social forces in this country.

CHAPTER THREE

DECISION MAKING AT THE NATIONAL LEVEL

DON PAARLBERG

ALL AROUND the world nations are reacting against the tide that carries us so rapidly toward urbanization. The Peruvian government tries to create new opportunities in the high plains of the Andes, so as to check the flow of people to Lima. Pakistan moves its capital to the interior of the country in an effort to broaden the geographic base of development. Brazil does the same. Turkey and Australia did so years ago. The Soviet Union increasingly builds its new plants in the rural areas rather than in the established industrial centers. The Israelis bring new nonfarm enterprises into the kibbutz, their cooperative farming system. In Malaysia a rural development program has been initiated to provide new amenities and opportunities in the countryside. Western Europe is engaged in a program that simultaneously increases the efficiency of agricultural production and provides off-farm employment opportunities for rural people. In southern Africa industrial jobs are being created in homeland areas, intended to check the flow of population to the great cities.

In the United States the rural development program, a cooperative effort supported by various departments of government, has grown from very small beginnings to a total of about $20 billion ($2.7 billion of it from the Department of Agriculture) in fifteen years of organized existence. The Congress will further increase this outlay.

These undertakings have not thus far checked the flow of people to the great cities nor redressed the disadvantages of rural people. In the United States 70 percent of the people live on 2 percent of the land. Rural areas contain one-third of the country's population;

DON PAARLBERG is Director of Agricultural Economics, USDA, Washington, D.C.

but they contain half the poverty, almost two-thirds of the substandard housing, and receive only one-fourth of the income.

Why this worldwide effort to check the trend toward urbanization? The reasons vary with time and place. These are the major ones:

The cities have become too large and congested, greatly increasing the cost of living and of doing business.

The countryside is being depopulated; in some areas the population has fallen below the level at which needed public services can economically be provided.

Overcrowding in the cities leads to lawlessness and disorder.

Considerations of equity argue for services to rural people comparable with those provided to people in the cities.

It is in the interest of national defense that the new increments of industry be located away from present manufacturing centers.

Excessive concentration of people in limited areas places great stress on the environment.

Some desirable noneconomic qualities in rural living would be lost if we were to continue the trend toward urbanization.

The effort to place a conscious check on the drift to the cities is new in public policy. For many years the United States has not had an enunciated policy with respect to the distribution of population; but we developed practices, attitudes, and habits that unconsciously carried us toward urbanization. We mechanized our farms, with the help of governmental research and development. We built most of our job opportunities in or near urban areas rather than in the countryside, where existing jobs were being closed out. Most of the social services we put in the cities: welfare, hospitals, education, government facilities, and entertainment. While many of our leaders continued using the rhetoric of agrarianism and agricultural fundamentalism, most of the things we actually did were contrary to agrarian principles.

There developed, in fact, a kind of urban fundamentalism. Some agricultural economists, aware of the errors of physiocratic thought and resultant agrarian beliefs, swung over to acquiesce in or even to advocate exodus from the farm and mass migration to the cities. There was a widely prevalent view that the urbanizing trend was both desirable and inevitable. We were carried along by the assumption made in theoretical economics that adjustments would be intelligent, instantaneous, and frictionless. These views are now being questioned—even challenged. Some would say they are being refuted.

The idea of rural development is often wrongly posed as a centrally designed blueprint based on certain stated goals as to the number of farms we should have and the percentage of our population that should live in rural areas. It is wrongly represented as a new, stated population policy, coming into a vacuum where no policy previously existed.

Rural development is a widening of the range of choice for rural people. So long as most of the increments of opportunity were built in the urban areas and farm jobs were diminishing, rural people had a very limited range of choice. If the various doors of opportunity are opened wider, the people themselves will select the door of their choice and will choose wisely. The task of rural development is to help the people achieve the goals to which they themselves aspire. We have had in the past an implicit policy that drove rural people to the cities; what is now proposed is an explicit policy that gives them a choice.

Rural development is not necessarily synonymous with economic development. The developmental process is more than just economic; it is also social, political, and esthetic. It is regrettable that the various social disciplines have contributed so unevenly to the understanding of this problem.

RESEARCH OF A DIFFERENT KIND. When rural development concepts began to take conscious form about fifteen years ago, they appeared in what might be called a microeconomic context: How do we find new enterprises for the small farm? How do we get a new industrial plant to build in a particular location? How can we get water, power, sewer, or better telephone service for a rural community? Research work in rural development was understandably intended to answer these questions.

Now questions of a macroeconomic sort are being asked, and they require research of a different kind. In macro terms, an irrigation project or a new farm enterprise in Region A may increase agricultural opportunities there, but with the price objectives specified in legislative programs, it will diminish opportunities in Region B. In a macro sense, nothing is gained if the new industrial plant locates at Podunk rather than at Compost Corners. Grantsmanship may help obtain a government project for a particular location, but with limited resources assistance is correspondingly reduced elsewhere.

In the arena of public policy we now see macro concepts emerging along with micro. The country is concerned with achieving a better rural-urban balance in a macro sense rather than trying to referee the contest as to who gets the limited available help in a micro setting.

If change has come faster than the researchers anticipated, this is not new. The same was true in the general field of economics. We first used micro concepts in trying to overcome the Great Depression, a phenomenon of macro nature. The same thing was true with regard to agricultural economics; that discipline was almost exclusively micro and entrepreneurial for the first forty years of its life and began to take account of macro concepts only recently. Some of our farm programs illustrate the error of carrying micro concepts into a macro setting or of undertaking actions based on macro concepts that were not carefully developed.

Researchers must anticipate needs, an undertaking so difficult that if they fail they should be forgiven. What is unforgivable is failure to respond to a need after it becomes identifiable.

APPROPRIATE MACRO RESEARCH. I shall now attempt something very bold, difficult, and hazardous—to suggest some appropriate macro research ventures. These undertakings would require competence in fields other than economics and would call for an understanding of things urban as well as rural.

Would the public benefit from a reduction in the concentration of our population?

What utilities and disutilities are there in providing public service to communities of various population densities?

As evidenced by our actions, how do people rate the social and esthetic values of rural compared with urban living?

What stress is placed on our soil, water, and air resources by various concentrations of population in various settings?

Is the conventional wisdom regarding plant location still valid? Is it as important to be close to raw materials and to markets as we have long thought?

What institutional arrangements encourage the concentration of population, and what are the obstacles to decentralization?

At what point and under what circumstances does the proximity of other people begin to have an adverse psychological effect on the individual and on society? (We seem to know far more about this as it relates to pigs and chickens than we do as it relates to people.)

What might be the costs and benefits of inducing a million people to live and work in a rural rather than in an urban setting?

Taking the best information presently available, what might constitute a rough optimum rural-urban population balance?

Some of these very tough questions have been addressed in part. Some of them probably are not researchable. But at the national level these questions are being asked and decisions are being made. Researchers are capable of shedding more light on these matters than they have in the past. They could at least provide a measure of our present ignorance, which in itself would be helpful.

I do not suggest that we neglect the more traditional micro studies. A great mistake occurred some years ago when the individual economist was led to feel that the issue between micro and macro economics was a zero sum game—that to the degree that macro economics had merit, the merit of micro economics was correspondingly diminished, and vice versa. On the contrary, both have merit. Macro economic aggregates do not leap into being by magically transcending the individual units of which they are composed. Even if the initiating forces are instituted by a national program, nothing really happens until individual persons make individual decisions. To look at totals without reference to their components is as inadequate as to look at individual units without reference to their sum.

What research is needed in the micro area? Here we need to take stock, to "research the research" and draw from it whatever principles we can. This need becomes more urgent as programs expand and decisions are taken. We have been doing a great many pieces of research, the meanings of which should be summarized. It is time to do for research in rural development what John D. Black once did for research in farm management; he pulled together the work of many people, some of them his own students, into a body of principles.

Tom Cowden, Assistant Secretary of Agriculture for Rural Development and Natural Resources, asks this question: "Can you provide, from your research, enough hard information to make a 45-minute talk on what it takes to get jobs in rural America?" Perhaps a reexamination of what we have already learned would provide a better answer than the launching of yet more individual new studies.

Bill Motes, Director of the Economic Development Division of our Economic Research Service, attempted to summarize our existing knowledge, condensed as follows:

There is great diversity in the condition, rate of growth, and potential for development of rural areas.
Thus rural development covers a range of problems, not just one. They must be faced on the basis of the special characteristics of each region or area.

Area development is synergistic.
This situation ensures that growing economic centers have increasing advantages, or frequently appear to have from the point of view of the

industrial decision maker. It also means that declining areas find themselves on a treadmill of increasing costs and declining services. The easiest time to stop area decline is before it begins. The further an area is from economic activity physically and the longer it is left, the more expensive and difficult the remedy will be.

[Bill Motes's observation appears to be contrary to the assumptions of economic theory, which postulate equilibrating rather than divergent development patterns. I think this observation is in large measure correct, and that our optimistic assumptions regarding the adjustment process have sometimes served as a convenient rationale for inaction. On the other hand, there must be some equilibrating forces or the diverging trends would go on forever, which they do not do.]

Successful remedial development must depend primarily on private economic investment.

Incentive-oriented efforts have the most good things going for them. Public investment can help provide incentives for private investment, but most programs have been focused on some average community, with a resulting bonanza for the growing community and little or no help for all those farther out.

Remedial development is costly and slow.

Remedial development means changing the economic climate of a region or an area. A long-established trend is very powerful and persistent. We should not expect to change the course of history by appropriating a few dollars, launching a few programs, and appointing a few people. Results of a lasting nature in three years are uncommon. Five to fifteen years is a more normal gestation period. Because so many other things happen, it is nearly impossible to trace cause-and-effect relationships.

Some patterns are discernible with regard to migration.

People do move when necessary and feasible, in order to improve their economic position.

People prefer to live near cities but not too near.

Programs to stop migration have thus far had little success, perhaps because they were not well designed.

More research is needed, but decisions will not wait for more research. We will have to go with what we have. In the language of systems analysis, we need to work on the feedback mechanism. Some of our research has found its way into the process, decisions have been made, experience has been obtained, and we must now examine the results in order to modify our research input for the next cycle.

Useful modifications are in two areas: the macro sector, where breeding and cross-breeding are required; and the micro sector, where we need the culling, sorting, screening, and refining of a crop already in hand rather than the indiscriminate seeding of yet more acreage to grow yet more bushels of the same old crop.

CHAPTER FOUR

DECISION MAKING AT STATE AND REGIONAL LEVELS

ALAN R. BIRD

IN THE United States the concept of rural development can be presented as a widening of choice not only for rural people but for all Americans, both as consumers and producers, by their productive involvement in the evolution in nonmetropolitan America of better places to live and work. These places will be an updated and adapted synthesis of the best of traditional rural and urban living.

REGIONAL DEVELOPMENT. We are familiar with such regions as the Cutover, the Dust Bowl, the Delta, and others. They tend to connote large areas with a common resource base, typically areas with resource problems due to past misuse or abuse of natural resources or other imbalances between man and nature. Often resident families and individuals have decided to move elsewhere, and the major public decision making has been the development of federal programs for remedial purposes. State and regional decision making commonly includes reacting to federal rules in search of extra public funds—grantsmanship if you will.

Also at the multistate level, regional planning and decision making have resulted in development of major federally sponsored public works by the Corps of Engineers and other groups. This public works thrust has been expanded through joint federal-state decision making in relation to the Appalachian region and the so-called "Title V Regions" (such as New England, Upper Great Lakes, and Four Corners), authorized under Title V of the Public Works and Economic

ALAN R. BIRD is Deputy Director, Economic Development Division, Economic Research Service, USDA, Washington, D.C.

Development Act of 1965 and its amendments. Other programs have gradually been added to try to round out the public works thrust into a more balanced development effort.

MULTICOUNTY LEVEL. At the multicounty level, decision making has commonly been a response to so-called "HUD 701" planning money (funds for state planning from the Department of Housing and Urban Development) and a further requirement from the federal Office of Management and Budgeting (OMB) that applications for federal grants and loans be cleared by substate organizations designated by the respective governors. Nonetheless, federal sponsorship of multicounty regions is now diverse and widespread. Notable are the Resource Conservation and Development Districts sponsored by the USDA, the areas involved in Concerted Services Projects for manpower development and training under multiagency sponsorship, the Economic Development Districts sponsored by the Economic Development Administration, and the local development districts sponsored by the Appalachian Regional Commission and cooperating states. A new demonstration program of the Department of Transportation involving the development of projects in relation to identified rural growth centers also can be expected to reinforce the notion of local areas or regions as planning and programming units for development. Table 4.1 summarizes the most recent numbers we have on the distribution of selected types of districts by state.

The multicounty planning and development regions can be thought of as building blocks for state and multistate regional programs. Under present Title V commissions, the precedent is well established for regional programs to be evolved from state proposals, which in turn may include proposals to deal with common problems of parts of participating states. States propose and the commissions (including joint federal-state representation) dispose. Legislation regarding these commissions already authorizes them to recognize and work with such districts or areas as the multicounty regions. This trend is a natural, pragmatic evolution and seems to strengthen the multicounty region as a central continuing unit for analysis and evolution of development programs and policies.

Multicounty regions also have significant state and local sponsorship. The regions served by the Area Planning and Development Commissions of Georgia are a notable precedent. So, on a more limited basis, are the widespread efforts at school consolidation. Thus multicounty regions offer promise of decision making through more direct involvement and commitment of local people than do larger regions. Generally, individual counties and towns offer promise of still more local decision making coupled with more direct and identi-

TABLE 4.1. Principal Planning and Development Districts of the United States by States, May, 1972

State	Planning and Development Districts	Economic Development Districts	Council of Government	Resource Conservation and Development	HUD Funded[d]
Ala.	12	2	3[a]	2	7
Alaska	...	...	...	...	...
Ariz.	6	...	3	3	...
Ark.	8	8[c]	3[a]	4[a]	9
Calif.	10	4[c]	4	1[a]	4
Colo.	12	1	2[a]	3	...
Conn.	15	...	6	1	6
Del.	...	1[a]	...	1	...
Fla.	10	2[c]	...	2	3
Ga.	18	12	4[a]	4	15
Hawaii	...	...	...	1[a]	...
Idaho	6[b]	3[ac]	4[a]	4[a]	4
Ill.	7	2	4[a]	2	5
Ind.	14	1	4[a]	2	...
Iowa	16	...	4[a]	3	...
Kans.	11	2[c]	3[a]	3	...
Ky.	15	11[c]	4[a]	2	6
La.	8	5	3	3	3
Maine	8[b]	1[a]	1[a]	2	6
Md.	7[b]	1	2	1	2
Mass.	12	1[c]	...	1	3
Mich.	13	7[c]	3[a]	2	5
Minn.	12	3[c]	5[a]	2	...
Miss.	10	10[c]	2[a]	3	8
Mo.	20[b]	4	21[a]	2	15
Mont.	12[b]	3	...	2	...
Nebr.	26	...	2[a]	1	1
Nev.	7[b]	...	1	2[a]	2
N.H.	17	1[a]	...	1	5
N.J.	...	...	2[a]	...	...
N.M.	6	2[c]	2	2	5
N.Y.	13	3[c]	...	2	3
N.C.	17	6[c]	9	2	7
N.D.	8[b]	...	1[a]	1	...
Ohio	12[b]	2	14[a]	3	...
Okla.	11	6[ac]	5[a]	3	1
Oreg.	14	4[ac]	14[a]	2	7
Pa.	13	3[c]	2	2	1
R.I.	...	...	...	1	...
S.C.	10	5	1[a]	3[a]	7
S.D.	6	...	2[a]	2	1[a]
Tenn.	9	7[ac]	5[a]	2	5[a]
Tex.	24	9[c]	24[a]	4	3
Utah	8	3[c]	6	1[a]	1[a]
Vt.	14	1[a]	...	1[a]	14[a]
Va.	22	5[ac]	1[a]	1[a]	2[a]
Wash.	13	5[ac]	4	2[a]	6
W. Va.	11	6[c]	...	4[a]	...
Wis.	8	1	2[a]	...	3
Wyo.	...	...	...	3[a]	1
Total	531	147	160	97	176

SOURCE: Development District Information System (DDIS), Economic Development Division, ERS, USDA, Washington, D.C. 20250.

[a] Includes one or more interstate district(s) in the count for each participating state. Thus, some of the columns do not add to the U.S. total. [b] Tentative. [c] Includes some authorized and/or funded as well as all officially designated. [d] May be a Planning and Development District, an EDD, COG, RC & D or other type of district.

fiable local government. Meaningful study of decision making at the multicounty level is likely to involve parallel and interrelated study of decision making for constituent communities.

Both the diverse origins and widespread recognition of these multicounty regions, districts, or areas make them fitting candidates for further study by researchers in land-grant institutions. Enough multicounty regions have now been designated to permit some systematic comparisons of their characteristics. As of March 1972, 487 such districts had been designated for 30 states, and a virtually complete districting of the United States with 500–600 such designations seems to be a feasible expectation (Fig. 4.1). These areas may be classified into a finite number of meaningful types such as the Great Plains, where for the most part continuing population sparsity and some outmigration can be expected, and the Southeast with continuing relatively dense settlement in spite of gross outmigration.

Multicounty regions make "economic sense" in that they are functional economic areas. In principle, it seems reasonable to postulate that an example of an adequately developed area or region would be one with a moderate-sized central city of about 50,000 and a hinterland or surrounding area within convenient commuting distance (a drive of one hour). These areas might be economically and socially interdependent so that a high proportion of hinterland residents commute to the city and those beyond that fringe tend to migrate to the city. This image of a region with a central city or "growth center" as the major source of jobs and income for residents of both the city and its rural hinterland is implied in the writings of Niles Hansen[1] and geographers such as Brian Berry[2] as well as in legislation (such as Title IV of the Public Works and Economic Development Act of 1965 which first authorized so-called "growth centers" associated with Economic Development Districts).

The functional economic area embodies one view of what a multicounty region should be like if it is adequately developed. It implies a dominant economic and social complementarity among residents of adjoining local government jurisdictions that is not adequately established empirically. For example, the commuting fields used by Berry in delineating regions comprise the farthest extent to which anyone commuted to the metropolitan area in question in one particular week enumerated by the census. Thus they extend far beyond the points from which any meaningful amount of regular daily commuting is feasible.

A few more reasons for critically studying the possible role of a

1. Niles M. Hansen, *Rural Poverty and the Urban Crisis* (Indiana Univ. Press, 1970), p. 353.
2. Brian J. L. Berry et al., "Commuting Fields of Central Cities and Counties and Functional Economic Areas of the United States," Social Science Research Council Committee on Areas for Social and Economic Statistics (Univ. Calif., April 1967).

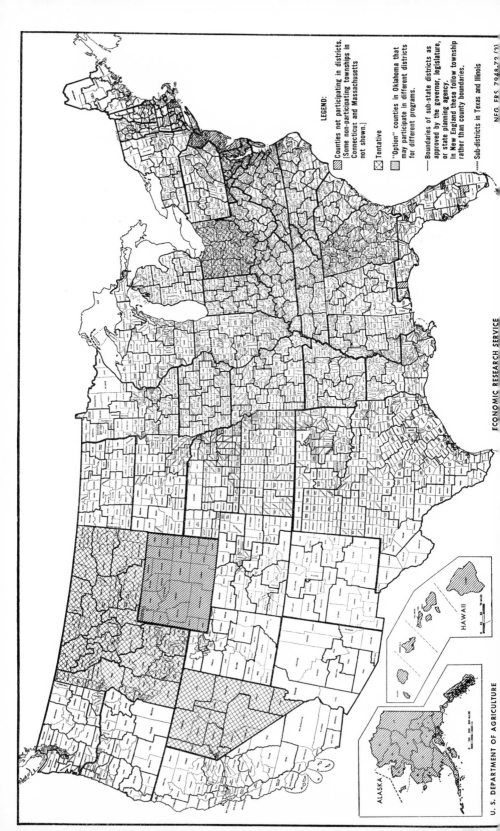

ECONOMIC RESEARCH SERVICE

NEG ERS 7948-72 (3)

U. S. DEPARTMENT OF AGRICULTURE

ALASKA

HAWAII

"growth center" and for shunning any unwarranted stereotyping of the functions of parts of a multicounty region are the following:

1. Nonmetropolitan areas in the South provided 42 percent of the manufacturing jobs in the region in 1960 and gained 753,000 such jobs (over half the total for the region) by 1970. These same nonmetropolitan areas employed only 25 percent of the construction workers in the South in 1960 but accounted for 33 percent of the construction employment gains in 1960–70. This performance varied greatly among counties in the region and seemed to be associated with a multiplicity of factors.[3]

2. In 1960 over 40 million nonmetropolitan residents lived in counties from which less than 5 percent of the workers commuted to any metropolitan destination—central city, suburbs, or outlying ring. This was two-thirds of the nonmetropolitan population.[4]

3. While many rural areas continued to lose population in the 1960s, many with little or no direct access to metropolitan areas did not. For example, a 25-county area in northwestern Arkansas included only two counties that gained in population during the 1950s, and the area experienced an overall population decline of 9 percent. By contrast, from 1960 to 1970 only two counties lost population, and the area had an overall gain of 19 percent.[5]

4. It is plausible to expect that many communities advance as much in competition as in cooperation with their neighbors. Problems of pollution, school systems, welfare, and many other social and economic burdens may be "dumped" on adjoining communities.

5. There is no adequately articulated and widely accepted body of knowledge on what makes an area or a region grow. Perhaps the dominant implied consensus is that a local economy is inherently more open and otherwise complicated and less understood than the national economy.[6] Given this state of knowledge (or ignorance), it seems best to accept multicounty regions as arbitrary and potentially relevant entities and explore their respective development potentials and implied and observed decision-making needs, including the needs of local areas and groups contained in these regions. Implications for boundary changes, among other things, could emerge from these pragmatic analyses.

---

3. Claude C. Haren, "Employment, Population and Income Growth in the South's Metro-Nonmetro Areas, 1960–70," EDD, ERS, USDA.
4. Calvin Beale, "Population and Migration Trends in Rural and Nonmetropolitan Areas" (Statement to Committee on Government Operations, U.S. Senate, Washington, D.C., April 1971), and personal communication.
5. Beale, "Population and Migration Trends."
6. Alan R. Bird, "Area Development—Status, Potential and Needs for Adequate Research Support," paper presented at National Area Development Institute, Spindletop Research, Lexington, Ky.

Although many kinds and sizes of regions can be identified, it would be most fruitful if extra research on rural development decision making at state and regional levels focused mainly on multicounty regions, particularly those designated by the respective states for overall development and planning purposes. This arbitrary judgment recognizes the large number of such districts already established, their varied origins, and the presence of some state initiative as well as federal incentives in their designation and operation. It also recognizes their limited conceptual, empirical, and legal underpinnings and the implied need for many interrelated pragmatic studies of decision making at multicounty and various sub- and supraregional levels. The essential feature of the regional decision-making process is not geographic or physical; on the contrary, it is the participation of two or more relatively independent public decision-making units in the solution of significant problems of local people.

REGIONAL RESEARCH VS. FARM-ORIENTED RESEARCH.

The scope for relevant research on rural development—even on just decision making at the regional level—is potentially infinite. Accordingly, a selective approach appears to be needed. The multicounty region should be the primary unit of focus of a substantial number of researchers in several disciplines. Part of this research would focus on decision making at this regional level as well as at the related state level and for the various local units (counties, cities, etc.) participating in the region. Researchers studying this phenomenon would be employed by federal, regional, state, and local public agencies as well as some private organizations and interest groups such as utility companies, banks, and national associations.

This primary focus on the multicounty region would correspond to the traditional focus of many agricultural economists on the farm as the key unit of description and analysis. However, the decision-making unit for a typical multicounty region is not nearly as well identified nor as compact and standardized as in the case of a farm. Traditionally, farm management specialists and production economists have focused on problems of identifying least-cost combinations for producing a given output or ways of maximizing output from a given bundle of resources. Related specialists have studied national and subnational policy and program implications for this or that change in production methods or technological breakthrough. Others have studied institutional conditions related to farm production, changes in farm size, and other features of the national farm policy; still others have analyzed performance and structure of related product and factor markets.

There is a similar though much more urgent and demanding need to evolve groups of specialists to study the program and policy implications at both national and subnational levels as they relate to changing socioeconomic conditions and related decision making in multicounty regions. And there is an obvious parallel need for studying institutional and marketing aspects of these regions.

Region-oriented research is much more difficult and challenging than farm-oriented research, and the initial base of first-hand experience and organized knowledge is much less. The problems that demand study in a region are typically much more controversial and the solutions less obvious. Thus research will likely be more fruitful if it involves a concentration of interrelated studies on specific regions and types of regions.

In the case of farm-oriented research, examples of successful farming operations are fairly plentiful. In the case of region-oriented research, it is not clear whether there is an adequate success story in each part of the country or not. In fact, one of the likely objectives of this research is to aid in the synthesis of new forms of regions that comprise interrelated communities that together have more advantages of traditional rural and urban living and fewer disadvantages.

At a lower level, relatively myopic research that serves what appear to be eminently practical community needs may actually create new community problems in much the same way that our previous penchant for increasingly efficient production of more food and fiber has exacerbated the economic and social adjustment problems of small farmers, farm workers, and businessmen and public officials of small towns. To the extent that we tend to accept a multicounty region uncritically as a unit of program analysis, development, and execution, there is a danger we may assume simplistic goals and related partial or oversimplified means of attainment of these goals.

The standard simplistic formula for rural development is to "get more jobs out there." This formula leads to emphasis on industrialization, typically through extra public programs of grants and loans plus technical assistance and some manpower training. This approach deserves questioning on several grounds. First, in endorsing this industrialization approach, are we in effect adopting the "definitional approach" to rural development? If a rural area is economically disadvantaged, will industrialization solve its problems? Indeed, if we pursue this policy far enough, we may advance the area so that it obtains levels of air, water, and noise pollution; traffic congestion; and crime as well as cultural and recreational services that match those of present major industrialized areas.

A further and relevant problem of the industrialization approach is that the areas deemed eligible for public assistance are typically the most economically disadvantaged, with relatively low income levels and relatively high rates of unemployment and underemployment. As part of the requirements for public assistance in industrialization, these communities usually are required to provide some matching money, and they are the communities least likely to have these funds. Furthermore, planning requirements of the sponsoring agencies are very demanding; these communities are least likely to be able to staff these planning activities with their own personnel.

Perhaps the greatest difficulty with this industrialization approach to rural development is that no one has yet adequately documented that successful or preferable communities have succeeded through industrialization, whereas successful commercial farms are easily identifiable. There may in fact be some successes, and a high priority might well be set on searching out and adequately documenting these cases for the benefit of all. However, it is doubtful that we shall easily discover these modern utopias. On the empirical side, the fragmentary evidence afforded by recent Gallup polls is that most people prefer "rural living." But continuing outmigration from rural areas and continuing commentary on the inadequate development status of these areas cause many to question what it is that people really prefer as a place of residence and a life style.

For some decades and perhaps with increasing rigor and insistence, we have identified maximizing farm income as an assumed, almost all-consuming goal of the farm unit. The farm, we say impatiently, is a business and must be analyzed as a business. Surely it is more than a business, but we imply that the farm family attains an improved and preferable way of life in accordance with its increase in money income. In regional or area development, economists and others have tended to opt for a broader spectrum of initial goals for a region or area. At a recent meeting of the Council of the National Area Development Institute the following set of goals for all citizens of a region or area was drawn up:[7]

1. Opportunity to increase money income, with commensurate participation in the labor force, and access to a socially acceptable guaranteed minimum income or its equivalent.
2. Opportunity for both children and adults to earn a generally acceptable high school diploma and its implied opportunities.
3. Access to medical, dental, and other health services—at least those normally provided by general practitioners in medicine and dentistry, but ideally including those of pediatricians, obstetricians and gynecologists, orthopedic surgeons, orthodontists, X-ray and normal supporting laboratory diagnostic and treatment services, and pharmaceutical services.
4. Access to a clean, safe, reliable water supply and related sewage and waste disposal (preferably on a community basis) and ade-

7. A similar paper was presented by Archibald Haller, "What constitutes quality of living?" *Quality of Rural Living* (Proceedings of a Workshop, National Academy of Sciences, Washington, D.C., 1971), pp. 3–6.

quate protection from other hazards of environmental pollution.
5. Adequate communication, at least a telephone or two-way radio.
6. Adequate housing including running water, at least one bathroom, and a normally equipped kitchen as well as power (individual or community supply) for heating, lighting, and cooling.
7. Minimal nutrition and clothing, or the income required to provide them.
8. Access, by normal mode under normal travel conditions, to supplementary community facilities and services widely accepted as part of modern living (such as restaurants and retail stores customarily providing a wide range of goods and services).
9. Access to library services permitting frequent exchange of books.
10. Access to outdoor recreation facilities and services—at least sufficient to allow all children the opportunity to learn to swim.
11. Public safety services and facilities including police, fire, ambulance, and disaster services such that all residents enjoy security of person and property.
12. Access to public information (including both newspapers and magazines) and continuing objective information on local economic and social conditions, employment and training opportunities, and needs in relation to national conditions and those in adjoining areas and other like areas.
13. Freedom and opportunity to worship and to participate in normal democratic processes of government, including voluntary organizations.
14. Opportunity to live in a community and in a work environment that is increasingly satisfying from an esthetic viewpoint, including the development or preservation of an area identity that involves some unique positive attributes.

To describe each of these items in sufficiently meaningful detail would probably take a minimum of three or four variables for a total of about 50. Items might well need to be specified also with respect to perhaps three income groups, some ethnic groups, various residence groups (county A or B), and industry groups (including farm). Thus it would not be surprising if some 300 items were needed to specify a first approximation to goals for a particular region. Of course some intercorrelations will occur among these items. Still, the potential complexity facing the rural development microanalyst is awesome.

In contrast to farm-centered studies, the number of decision makers is much greater, and the identity of the major decision makers can be expected to vary from decision to decision. And of course both ways of making a decision and means of carrying it out can be expected to be similarly complex and volatile.

**IMPLIED APPROACHES TO RESEARCH ON DECISION MAK-
ING.** What then are the implications for research on decision
making at state and regional levels? The size and complexity of
the research challenge point to the need for concentrated team efforts
in which researchers of various backgrounds communicate continually
both with one another and with their clientele.[8] The North Central
Regional Center for Rural Development is a promising enabling instrument for this. However, a likely parallel need is the creation of
Departments of Agricultural and Development Economics, although
the organizational mode to enable the needed major new emphasis
on rural development will likely vary with the traditions and other
characteristics of various parent institutions. In such a transitional
phase equal weight might be given to development and agriculture,
whatever this organizational mode.

As researchers relate to their clientele, more initial progress
might be made by concentrating a group of studies on an individual
"typical" region and the communities contained in it rather than by
scattering individual studies across many regions. The input required
for a series of successful studies in the one region is likely to be large
relative to the research resources available, and there is no guarantee
of immediate success. Accordingly, the temptation will be great to
concentrate these limited resources on macro or policy studies. Coefficients and the identification of meaningful constraints and options
derived from regional decision-making studies will probably often be
necessary inputs to enable meaningful macro studies to be made.
These two kinds of studies are likely to be more complementary than
competitive.

Moreover, successful researchers are likely to be a new breed
who combine in each individual the best technical qualities of a successful researcher and a missionary zeal for solving priority problems. Many already feel that the one individual must combine research and extension capabilities; others question the feasibility of
finding or developing a sufficient number of individuals with such a
range of capabilities. There is as yet little definitive material to "extend," and dialogues with community leaders need to stress a joint
process of learning and discovery. Productive approaches will likely
oscillate between serendipity and scientific progress in the land-grant
tradition of expanded numerical analysis and insistence on practical
applications.

Any research on regional problems of rural development will be
conducted in the context of current and expected national economic,
social, and technological conditions, programs, and policies. Research-

---

8. Interdisciplinary efforts are demanding and not automatically successful.
   The composition and working arrangements necessary for a successful team
   effort are not matters of wide agreement. For a relevant recent commentary, see William Alonso, "Interpretation: Beyond the inter-disciplinary
   approach to planning," *AIP Journal* (May 1971), pp. 169–73.

ers at state and regional levels cannot ignore the implications of this national context. Research must point to needed joint resolution of problems with this larger environment. Major differentials among states in welfare payment rates and eligibility conditions and the mysteries and variability of the federal budgeting process and related administrative decisions on opening, closing, and operating both federal installations and local units of national corporations are examples of conditions that can mean life or death to an individual community.

Even in community problems directly related to agriculture there appears to be much scope for researchers to analyze possible improvements in community adjustment options that imply needed improvements in federal programs. What are the possibilities and implications, for example, of excluding from liability for capital gains taxes the sales of small farms or parcels of land to farmers who seek to consolidate land to form an efficient modern unit?[9] What programs can be devised to enable the relocation of businessmen from towns now made remote or redundant by modernized farm production to sites where their businesses can still be profitably pursued? What programs and policies will best enable communities to adjust to a further concentrated impact due to technological and related institutional change, such as may be occurring in some areas due to tobacco mechanization, the demise of the migrant farm worker, and the unionization and professionalization of farm workers?

The development orientation envisaged by a region addressing itself to a comprehensive set of goals subsumes antipoverty activities. Perennial discussion persists on the income distributional and equity aspects of development. Development projects are frequently criticized because most of their payrolls go to workers not officially designated as "poor" or "disadvantaged." They may also be criticized because some of the jobs so generated yield incomes only just above some customary poverty level. The projects so criticized are often in economically disadvantaged regions that have a disproportionate share of the poor and a likely limited resource base. Is it reasonable, likely, or fair that such a region can devise and implement projects to upgrade all its own residents, even with outside financial and technical assistance? The development prospects of such a region would be much brighter if its poverty burden were equalized with those of other regions. Implied necessary resource adjustments would likely include accelerated and assisted outmigration of many more poor residents and inmigration—through the incentive of economic and social opportunities—of a core group of people of relatively high income, relatively skilled and highly trained. Each region could evolve a range of needed job and training opportunities.

9. Alan R. Bird, "Improving the Transfer of Farm Real Estate in the Saginaw Valley and Thumb Area of Michigan," Quart. Bull. Mich. Agr. Exp. Sta. (Feb. 1961), 43(3):482–90.

The ability of a region to attract its share of highly productive inmigrants on a continuing basis may turn out to be the first consideration—the key point of orientation to regional and rural development. Our doctrinaire heritage includes something called "economic base theory." A pedestrian explanation of this theory would be that communities, like people, must have something to sell the outside world if they are to succeed or even survive.

If chronically disadvantaged regions (including those that are mainly rural) are to advance economically and socially fast enough to close income and employment gaps and other gaps in levels of well-being relative to the nation, they will need to expand their sales to the nation very rapidly. A similar need applies to more advanced regions, if they are to maintain or advance their respective positions. To attain these advances, individual regions need to produce some share of the traditional goods and services demanded by the nation's consumers, private corporations, and public agencies. More than that apparently is needed, however. Although some regions may produce and market a sufficient volume of traditional goods and services at competitive prices to enable reasonable rates of development, many others will likely need to emphasize new goods and services, particularly those demanded by higher-income consumers and large and expanding corporations. Productive research might seek out possible options for particular regions and types of regions, taking account of both technological and social innovations.

How does research gear up to meet such a need? Apart from evolving needed new organizations and orientations, researchers must find ways to be more selective in subject matter and problem area priorities but less constrained in setting the terms of reference of particular studies that are undertaken.

Where do people really want to live and why? There probably is not any clear dichotomy of rural versus urban preferences. People do not live or even move to a place necessarily because they prefer this location. Locational policies of firms and public agencies deserve similar scrutiny, including a search of altruistic, perceptive, and crass components. Penetrating analyses of specific regions and public and private decision-making units contained in them will likely be needed to establish adequate guidance on locational preferences of either firms or individuals. These analyses might well relate to specific parts of the spectrum of regional goals already listed.

Impact or evaluation studies might be similarly broadened. For example, a series of ERS studies on industrialization in rural areas concentrated on income and employment impacts of particular projects.[10] Similar studies could include appraisal of a broader range of

---

10. John C. Crecink, "Rural Industrialization: Case Study of a Tissue Paper Mill in Pickens, Mississippi," AER 189, EDD, ERS, USDA (Sept. 1970),

impacts, in relation to a spectrum of goals such as the one listed above, and also be repeated periodically to document sequences of ensuing decisions in regional perspective.

A common problem of all regions—and one that probably has more variants than there are regions—is how to provide adequate and increasingly superior community services and facilities. To the extent feasible, analyses of economies and diseconomies of size in the provision of specific services and of possible externalities due to packaging of services may be helpful—even necessary. But researchers will benefit a specific region or type of region only if they can carry their analyses to the point of identifying and evaluating specific options that can and might confront regional decision makers.

Economists and other analysts have a continuing interest in analyzing community services and the role of the public sector in rural development. Much of the frustration stems from the perennial and unresolved question of how to measure the quality of public services.[11] Continuing attention to this question is needed. In the interim, some progress must be made in measuring trade-offs among packages of services that relate to specific sectors of the spectrum of goals listed above. More emphasis is needed in evaluating packages of services at the margin they relate to inmigrants of various skill and income levels, outmigrants, and other significant groups of regional residents.

One way of attaining the degree of relevance needed in research on decision making might be to start with a direct analysis of key decisions, then sift out significant decisions and analyze possible options against an overall list of regional goals and the need to integrate product and factor markets with corresponding national markets. Key regional decision makers would include both public officials (elected and appointed) and citizen leaders in voluntary organizations and particular firms and businesses—responsible people with a stake in the resulting action or inaction.

p. 12; Herbert Hoover, "Rural Industrialization in Kentucky: Case Study of a New Bedding Plant at Munfordville, Ky.," mimeo, ERS, USDA (May 1969), p. 18; Herbert Hoover, "Rural Industrialization in West Virginia: Case Study of a New Particle Board Plant in Braxton County, West Virginia," mimeo, ERS, USDA (May 1969), p. 18; Max F. Jordan, "Rural Industrialization in the Ozarks: Case Study of a New Shirt Plant at Gassville, Arkansas," AER 123, EDD, ERS, USDA (Oct. 1967), p. 37; Jackson V. McElveen, "Rural Industrialization in the Southeast Coastal Plain: Case Study of a New Brick Factory in Summerville, S.C." AER 174, EDD, ERS, USDA (Feb. 1970), p. 13.

11. S. M. Leadley (compiler), "Working Papers on Rural Community Services," Dept. Agr. Econ. and Rural Sociology, Pa. State Univ., Mar. 1972; Thomas F. Hady, "The Role of the Public Sector in Economic Development," mimeo, EDD, ERS, USDA (Feb. 1971), p. 7.

CHAPTER FIVE

DECISION MAKING AT THE COMMUNITY LEVEL

DON BROBERG

THE Resource Conservation and Development (RC&D) projects being conducted in 11 midwestern states are one way of implementing a rural development program. They are initiated and carried out by local people with the assistance of state and federal agencies under present program authorizations, including that contained in Sections 31 and 32 (e) of Title III of the Bankhead-Jones Farm Tenant Act of 1962 (Public Law 87-703) and the Soil Conservation Act of 1935 (Public Law 74-46). Leadership responsibility in the USDA for assistance to sponsors of RC&D projects has been assigned to the Soil Conservation Service by Secretary's Memorandum No. 1665.

These projects help people take better care of their natural resources and at the same time improve their community's economy. Locally initiated, sponsored, and governed, RC&D projects are based on the premise that people in the project areas can more fully develop their resource potentials; solve their resource problems; and meet their economic, environmental, and social needs through their own efforts if given encouragement and some help by public agencies.

The decision makers in an RC&D project are usually active in community affairs and serve on many other boards in their communities. Their participation in RC&D projects is usually their first experience in multicounty resource planning and development on a continuing basis.

As of February 1972, 98 such projects were authorized in the United States, representing all or parts of 630 counties in all states except New Jersey and Alaska. Applications are pending for an additional 61 projects involving all or parts of 332 counties. Most projects

DON BROBERG is Regional Resource Development Specialist, Midwest Regional Technical Service Center, Soil Conservation Service, Lincoln, Neb.

recently authorized are conterminous with substate planning regions and may cover one or more substate planning regions.

HOW PROJECTS FUNCTION.

HOW PROJECTS FUNCTION. The typical Resource Conservation and Development project covers four to eight counties in a predominantly rural area. It is cosponsored by legal entities including soil conservation districts and the county governments in the project area. Frequently other groups such as extension councils and city governments also cosponsor the project. If there is an organized planning commission in the area, it may be a cosponsor too. Civic groups, chambers of commerce, farm groups, service clubs, business organizations, and other groups are invited to endorse and support the project. The objective is to obtain a broad base of support for project action.

In a typical RC&D project, decision making occurs at three levels: decisions that affect the entire project area and priorities for action are made at the project (multicounty) level; other decisions are made at the county and community levels.

The decision-making body at the multicounty level is commonly called the RC&D Council. It is composed of representatives from each of the sponsoring organizations and includes others selected by the sponsors because of their interest in community development. The council is responsible for developing a project plan, which includes inventory data, the objectives of the project sponsors, problems and needs related to the development of resources, and proposed actions (project measures) to accomplish the objectives.

The council selects technical advisers (usually representative of state and federal agencies) to assist them in developing the project plan. The advisers can supply inventory data to the council regarding the amounts and kinds of resources in the project area and also interpret the data as they relate to the problems and opportunities for resource development. The RC&D Council establishes its objectives and goals for resource development and develops a list of project measures that, when implemented, installed, or established, will help these objectives. Each project measure must have a qualified local sponsor who is ready, willing, and able to do the job.

Project measures are developed in two ways: (1) the RC&D Council proposes an action and then finds a local unit of government or other organized group willing and able to carry it out. (2) Local units of government or organized groups submit proposals for project measures which they believe will help solve resource problems or develop a resource opportunity. These local government units usually are seeking assistance, technical and/or financial, from the RC&D Council to carry out the proposals.

Proposals range from developing a flowerbed in the town square to multimillion dollar irrigation projects, flood-prevention activities, papermills, and recreation enterprises. The proposals include information as to what is being proposed, how it will benefit the community, and what assistance is needed from the RC&D Council.

The council reviews each proposal in reference to the goals of the project. They establish a priority for action considering the extent to which the proposal will help them attain their goals and considering the economic, social, and political significance of the proposal. Councils usually do not have any legal authority and are like a planning commission in this respect. Therefore, they cannot stop a county or community from taking action on any proposal, nor can they force a county or community to take action on any proposal. They do have influence, particularly if federal funding is involved, and serve a very useful function in coordinating activities in the project area.

Since most RC&D projects cover more than one county, a decision-making body, usually called the County RC&D Committee, reviews each proposal as an intermediate step between the community and the project level. The committee considers each proposal in reference to the goals and objectives of the RC&D Council and other proposals submitted from their county and recommends a priority for action to the council for each proposal.

The planning and decision making constitute a continuous operation in RC&D projects. Plans for the development of the project area are prepared and printed from time to time and supplemented at least annually. New proposals are added, and some proposals are dropped if they do not appear to be feasible in the foreseeable future or if they would not contribute significantly to the goals and objectives of the project.

The planning and decision-making process described for RC&D project operations is not unique. Similar procedures can and probably are being used in other forms and organizations working in the field of rural development. Likewise, the problems the councils have in planning the development of a predominantly rural area probably exist for other forms of rural development organizations also.

These problems can be classified into three general groups:

1. What is the development status of the community now?
2. What should be done to improve the community?
3. Where should the improvements be located to be most effective?

Research is needed to develop methods of defining these problems in order to facilitate decision making.

PROBLEM INDICATORS. The first problem an RC&D Council faces is to get comprehensive knowledge of their project area. An overwhelming amount of statistical data is available, but what does it really mean in terms of social, economic, environmental, and political development? This is the first attempt for most rural decision makers to plan in a comprehensive manner, so the interpretations must be understandable in lay language. It would be most helpful if reliable indicators could be developed for rural decision makers to use to rate the present state of affairs in their community. The same system could then be used to measure progress (either plus or minus) as the development occurs over a period of years.

For example, what is a reliable indicator of the social well-being of a community? Is it the number of schools, the number of arrests, the number of civic clubs? What combination of factors can reliably indicate the social state of a community?

It would be preferable to rely on something other than census data because of the ten-year interval between census takings. It would also be preferable to have the indicator base compatible with census data to provide a check on the accuracy of the indicators. This check system would be comparable to using computers to predict the outcome of a major election or using information gained in an election to predict the outcome of future elections.

The same principle could be applied to indicators to measure the economic, environmental, and political status of the community. A rating for each of these four major areas would give an indication of the status of the community. For example, if the indicators show that a community is economically strong but environmentally weak, perhaps its economic strength is being gained at the expense of the environment. Therefore, resources may be needed to improve the environment. The reverse is probably more likely to be common in a rural area, so the question is, What environmental considerations are involved in any attempt to improve the economic well-being of the community?

The term "political status" is used here in the broad sense. Some indication of the political status might be the number of governmental jurisdictions operating in the community. How well are their actions coordinated by statute or by common understanding? How well are they adapted to implementing plans for rural development? Changing a political system even slightly creates controversy, but to ignore opportunities for improvement certainly limits the possibilities of meaningful development of rural areas.

Rural decision makers could proceed with more confidence to establish realistic objectives and goals if they had a better understanding of their community's problems.

COMMUNITY IMPROVEMENTS. The second group of problems relates to what should be done to improve the community. Research is needed to develop a method for classifying project measures according to their effect on the social, economic, environmental, and political development of the community.

For example, what will be the effect of the flowerbed in the town square compared to that of an irrigation development? The answer is rather obvious, but to what degree and how to measure it is the problem. What about a proposal for a home for juvenile delinquents compared to a pasture renovation program? What will be the effect of developing an outdoor recreation facility designed for 50,000 visitor-days annually?

Research is particularly needed to evaluate the social and environmental benefits and costs of each project measure. These benefits and costs seem to be difficult to express in terms of dollars. Some other unit of measure is needed that can express the presence or absence of a human life, a handful of soil, or a flock of geese northward bound on a spring morning.

An RC&D Council may have 200–600 proposals before them at any given time. A reliable system of classification would help rural decision makers decide which project measures should have the highest priority.

Most rural leaders agree that more job opportunities are needed in rural areas. A more specific research need is to identify those industries that can be decentralized into rural communities and whose peak labor demands are either compatible with peak labor demands in agriculture or can be adjusted to fit. Additional understanding of this subject would enable local decision makers to be more specific in their search for industrial development. Case studies may be a research approach to this need.

LAND USE PLANNING. The third group of problems relates to where improvements should be located. Most rural decision makers agree that some form of land use planning is needed, but there is no universal agreement on how rural land use planning should be done or who should do it. It is obvious that a feedlot should not be placed next to a recreational area, or that rural residences should not be permitted on soils that cannot be used for on-site sewage disposal, or that some kinds of construction should not be allowed in flood plains. The question is, To what extent should a landowner's rights be restricted or protected to benefit society as a whole?

The research need is to explore present methods of rural land use planning and zoning and their effect on the development of those rural areas. Case studies may be a method of approaching this need.

The problems that rural decision makers face are many and varied. It is difficult to precisely define these problems in terms of research needs. Generally, it appears that more research is needed to better define the comprehensive aspects of community planning and development. Research data are available on individual sectors of community development but not on methods of evaluating the community as a whole.

Planned rural development is a relatively new field; as the problems are better defined, we can logically expect better answers.

CHAPTER SIX

DECISION MAKING AT THE HOUSEHOLD LEVEL

RICHARD L. D. MORSE

THE HOUSEHOLD is the nucleus of our society. This is where the people are; unfortunately, too often it is where professionals are not!

Development connotes a *value* orientation, an affliction social scientists have prided themselves in avoiding. Thus rural development may present professional social scientists with having to make a choice between value-sterile professional academic pursuits and value commitments; the academic faculty will be forced to choose between "scholarly security" and "productive reality." An even greater burden of choice falls on administrators as they commit funds and select faculty willing to devote their professional life to rural development.

Values, then, pervade development. What are the criteria for progress? A related question is, Progress for whom? Is the goal of rural development to so develop and redirect the utilization of rural resources as to advance the quality of life of the (1) urban residents, (2) rural residents, or (3) both groups of citizens by helping improve the quality of living of the rural households in a manner that complements advancement in the quality of life for the urban residents?

Let us assume that rural development must have as its focus the advancement in the quality of rural living. This raises a third and practical question: How can programs that require support from urban-oriented legislatures be sold? Many urban people have grown suspicious of the commodity groups selling farm programs that fatten their own pockets under the pretext of helping the small farmers. If a genuine program of rural development is proposed, will it appear plausible to urban legislators and citizens?

A second assumption is that the type and style of household liv-

RICHARD L. D. MORSE is Professor and Head, Department of Family Economics, Kansas State University, Manhattan.

ing to be encouraged as a part of rural development is that of the nuclear family. Experiments in communal living attract publicity, but they have not proven to be the style of living to be encouraged under rural development. And, while vestiges of the rural extended family remain, reversal is not contemplated as a goal of rural development.

A third assumption is that the independently housed nuclear family is preferred to institutionalized living. This is particularly relevant in appraising housing and personal health care programs for the rural aged.

These assumptions, which probably represent the values held by the vast majority of people in mid-America, might become hypotheses and constitute a major research undertaking—namely, to discover the life style or styles of families that should be encouraged via rural development. There is a cause-and-effect relationship between rural development and family living. Family life patterns will be affected by rural development whether or not it is a stated policy. It follows, therefore, that any rural development proposal should include an analysis of its probable effect on family living patterns.

FAMILY LIFE CYCLE. All too often we think of families or households as comprising a mother and father and some children, not realizing that half the farm families in the United States currently have no children.[1] The child-bearing and rearing years take less than half of the family's life span, so rural development for family living must recognize the role of childless families.

Families are not static but are constantly undergoing change, so decision making varies according to the stage in the life cycle. The decisions made by a young couple with no children may differ greatly from those made by families with children. Furthermore, among childless families are those yet to have and those who have had children, and their outlooks will vary greatly. Also among older families are those who consider retirement as an opportunity to start a new career and those who view it as the last leg on the journey of life.

Rural development may be designed to contribute services that alter the parameters for decision making of families at different stages in the life cycle. For example, the type of recreation provided under rural development will have a differential effect on groups of families, depending on whether the emphasis is on youth or senior centers. A persistent question for research then is: What is the effect of various programs on the families at different stages of the life cycle?

1. U.S. Bureau of Census, P-20, No. 233, Feb. 1972, *Household and Family Characteristics: March 1971*, Table 1.

TIMES FACTOR. We often fail to recognize that decision making
of households is affected by the sequence of historical events experienced—the times in which the family lives. By reading the
rings of a cross-cut section of a tree one can interpret the environmental factors that prevailed at each stage in the growth of that tree.
Likewise families bear the scars of unemployment, wars, inflations,
and the boosts of prosperity. This became evident as we interpreted
the results of a statewide cross-sectional survey of 527 farm-operator
families in 1955. We were concerned with their provisions for financial security, and it was in this context that these families were viewed:

> Since 1895 (the year in which the first couple in the survey was
> married) Kansas people have experienced two world wars and the Korean
> conflict, suffered the farm depression of the 20s and the national depres-
> sion of the 30s, and more recently enjoyed the prosperity following
> World War II.
>
> To put these families in the perspective of history, the sixty families
> married between the years of 1905 and 1915 raised their children during
> World War I. Their children were likely to be marrying during the
> depression of the 30s and, by 1954, should have been in a position to
> provide emergency care for their parents. The forty-eight families formed
> during the period of 1916–20 and the forty-four families married in
> 1921–25 raised most of their children during the depression, and many
> of these children served in World War II. The sixty-one families formed
> from 1926 through 1930 raised their children in an economically de-
> pressed period. Although their children were too young to serve in World
> War II, they probably were eligible to serve in the Korean conflict.
> These children would have been starting their own families during a
> period of prosperity. The seventy-eight families formed during the
> period 1931–35 had young children during the depression but enjoyed the
> prosperity following World War II when their children's expenses were
> high; their children were of college age at the time of the survey. The
> seventy-nine families formed from 1936 through 1940, immediately prior
> to World War II, had their children during the war and enjoyed the
> postwar prosperity. Nearly all the children of these families were in-
> cluded in the survey, as well as the children of the seventy-eight families
> formed during the period 1941–45. These children were raised during
> war and postwar prosperity. The children of the fifty-two families formed
> during the period 1946–50 and of the eighteen families formed since
> 1950 were either of preschool age or in the lower grades at the time of
> the interview. Although the parents of these families were raised during
> the depression, their children have experienced only prosperity.[2]

Another observation is that an analysis of today's youth should
recognize that they are the first generation to be raised on a diet of
television and therefore will respond differently in years to come than
their predecessors at each chronological age or family life cycle stage.

2. Richard L. D. Morse, "Economic Status and Financial Security Provision of
    Kansas Farm-Operator Families, 1955," Dept. Family Econ., Kans. State
    Univ., 1965.

A better understanding of decision making of households is to be had if the data are considered not only in terms of the usual socio-economic variables such as income, age of family, and education but also in terms of the stage in life cycle and the times factor.

FAMILY ECONOMY. A discussion of decision making at the household level would be incomplete without taking some cognizance of the family as an economic unit.

The family is a small-scale enterprise which, by its very composition, cannot benefit from the economies of a large-scale operation. Its overhead costs are high in both durables and labor. The "new people" who have rediscovered communal living enjoy the economies of scale obtained by cutting down the durables overhead, but even for them the cost of fixed labor can be high. Furthermore, labor is unspecialized and usually untrained. Few of the tasks are so repetitiously performed as to encourage development of skill proficiency comparable to that attainable on the mass production line. The division of labor is such that usually the same person is a policy maker, manager, and performer; these roles are more often blended than distinct. Thus the household, never a self-sufficient unit and always dependent on outside assistance, now needs the expertise of specialists in such areas as health care, education, and law. That is, the family needs access to a large staff of professionals. The rural family is further disadvantaged by its residence in a diminishing community characterized by a lack of experts and specialized goods and services.

Rural development must recognize the high cost of services and develop ways to reduce the cost of these resources necessary for families. The Cooperative Extension Service for years recognized this and was the community consultant on a wide range of subjects. But more recently the high cost of specialized and needed services for rural living has been prohibitive, and lack of essential services has been a cause for the rural exodus. Thus the household, which admittedly is an uneconomic, high-cost unit, becomes even more costly in a rural setting. Furthermore, the elderly household, which requires more of the high-cost services of transportation and health care, is relatively important in rural areas. The question is one of developing mechanisms or changes in public policy to reduce the costs to the household unit.

RURAL-URBAN GAP. Since the economic problems of households arise primarily out of the gap between what the family desires and what it can buy, we should recognize the influence that mass media have on changing desires and that this commercially oriented and sponsored education originates in cities and reflects an urban orientation. The rural resident's concept of good living thus has grown much closer to that of the urban dweller. Through television the rural residents see the same ads and supposedly yearn for the same kinds of homes, washing machines, and makeup as the urban residents.[3]

Since the psychological factor is so important in goal setting—and goals are what drive us on—I suggest as a topic for research an analysis of media programming for its image portrayal of rural living. Is the best in rural living depicted? Or is Hee-Haw, shooting, cussin', use of poor grammar, and smokin' Marlboros the prevalent rural life scene? What aspects of rural America are worth preserving? Pride in rural living can be developed, but only if the desirable qualities can be identified and then promoted and advertised.

FAMILY FUNCTIONS. Decision making of the household relates to the five basic functions of the family: (1) to perpetuate the race, (2) to provide their economic support, (3) to give a satisfying and secure home life, (4) to prepare the child for adult self-discipline, and (5) to provide a buffer for the individual in a complex impersonal society. Of these, the most important to the interaction of rural development and family policy is reproduction. The fertility rate of the rural family has been high, higher than replacement levels. In fact fertility levels are inversely related to proximity to metropolitan centers. Rural America has been the Brooder House of America.[4]

Does America need these children? Can urban America absorb them any longer? Can rural America absorb them and also relieve the cities of their burgeoning population? What is the population planning policy for rural America? What are the capital requirements of raising a child in those rural American households that now no longer have a cow to milk or garden to provide low-cost nutritious foods?

Related questions for research range from the basics of motivational questions and attitudes toward family size to the specifics of availability and cost of family limitation methods and supplies. Furthermore, rural America, because of its knowledge and practice of genetic selection, might lead the country by its adaptation of this knowledge to limit the reproduction of the mentally and physically handicapped.

This concern for the quantity and quality of the population may

3. For further discussion, see Richard L. D. Morse, "The lengthening distance between the haves and the have-nots," *J. Home Economics*, Oct. 1967.
4. U.S. Bureau of Census, P-20, No. 203, *Fertility of the Population: January 1969*, Table 5.

seem to lie beyond the scope of rural development, but we must learn to think in broad terms. We need to think in macro terms and learn how to relate macro data to our own situations. Most of us adults were not so taught and hence are not prepared to think through social problems in this dual fashion, and we are not preparing our youth much better. We are likely to refrain from useful discussions of the role of government in relation to personal decisions on grounds that politics is involved and we assume that is beyond objective study. Unfortunately, youth may develop personal attitudes toward family planning that may be inconsistent with long-range social needs because they lack the perspective needed to make social judgments, particularly in such sensitive and critical matters as the quantity and quality of population. Too frequently the concept of government is either that it is not to be trusted or that it must be defended patriotically even at the sacrifice of young men. Unfortunately, most do not understand and appreciate the government they expend great effort to preserve.

The quality of rural living is directly related to how well the family performs its other basic functions. The family as an economic and social unit must provide basic minimum amounts of food, clothing, and housing; must provide security, love, warmth, and kindness; must prepare its children for independent and healthy family living; and must be ready to fortify and support one another in adversity.

As every parent knows, serious decision making is required in the raising of children. And after the children are gone, the adults must shift their focus from the children to themselves and think in terms of retraining for gainful employment, taking advantage of opportunities in continuing education, and preparing for living (consuming), especially in retirement years.

QUALITY OF RURAL LIVING: A CONSUMER VIEW. The quality of rural living depends partially on employment and money income needed to buy material goods, services, and financial security but also on whether the goods and services are available in the quality and quantity desired. A rural resident with money is poor if transportation services are unavailable and the auto insurance policy is canceled; he is poor and troubled if a homemaker or neighbor is not available to come in and help with even the simplest household routines or assist in administering personal health treatments; he is treated shabbily when sold false hopes, deceived into buying misrepresented goods or services, or abused into signing a financial contract that is collectable even if the seller disappears or if his product fails.

The importance of job development to enhance money incomes

is not denied, but mere job creation can create rural industrialization which should not be confused with rural development. The quality of rural development is directly related to the quality of housing, health services, insurance, financing, education, and other services available as well as the family's ability to be prudent and responsible consumers.

We should recognize the need for outside expertise in consumer rights and responsibilities[5] and restudy the consumer in rural America and the fulfillment of his rights as he exercises his responsibility of making decisions that are right for his family. A "restudy" is necessary because the sociological patterns have so shifted that the social taboos—the check-and-balance systems and social restraints of the small town—no longer hold. Customs which possibly had even greater force than the force of law have been discarded without adequate replacement. One example of this transition is the changing credit roles. The banker once served as the financial counselor for the community. Then it was difficult for a family to finance home repairs or buy encyclopedias from a disreputable dealer through the bank without the banker offering a word of caution if not refusing to make the loan. Today it is not unusual for a home repairman, book salesman, or other solicitor to call on rural residents and get their signature on sales credit contracts which the seller will then discount at a bank or finance company. The consumer will be required to make payments to the banker or finance company as holder of the contract even if the home repairs are unsatisfactory or the books are not delivered. If the consumer stops payment, the financier can sue for payment, taking as his defense what is known as the holder-in-due-course doctrine which says in effect, "Pay me, and if you have a complaint, go find the original seller." Farm families have been known to lose their homes and farms because an aluminum siding company which later went out of business made promises it did not fulfill. The United States government, which had bought these contracts from a finance company as an FHA home improvement loan, demanded payment.

Modern legislation would change the laws so as to make the buyer of the credit paper as responsible for the performance of the goods or services as the seller. The effect would be for the financier to return to his former role of checking on the reliability of the seller to perform satisfactorily before buying his credit contracts.

This is but one example of why there is special need not to neglect the consumer rights and responsibilities in rural development.

5. For further discussion see "The consumer moves from poison to truth," *J. Home Economics*, Apr. 1972.

Listed below are rights that are applicable throughout society, particularly as they relate to a rural development research project.

1. *Right to Safety*—No special problem for rural residents exists here except (a) there has been a tendency to exempt farmers from safety standards; (b) there is a need for improved communication with centers, such as poison control centers and product safety centers, especially for rural residents; and (c) inadequate standards for nursing homes have resulted in unsafe living for rural aged.
2. *Right to Be Informed*—This presents major problems for rural consumers. *Help Yourself,* published in Kansas by the Sedgwick County Attorney's Consumer Protection Division, is an example of a publication that should be available to all rural residents.[6] It describes the prevalent consumer frauds and tells how and where to complain. It also contains an index of all local, state, and national consumer agencies, cross-indexed with the major consumption areas.

   Inward WATS telephone lines to consumer dealers and consumer centers are needed to reduce the communication gap for rural residents. These have been used very successfully in Georgia as well as by companies such as American Motors, Whirlpool, and Travelers Insurance.
3. *Right to Choose*—This right is limited for rural residents in most consumption goods and services areas. Research is needed to assess how much choice a rural consumer has and how choice might be increased. What restraints are placed on competition from business foreign to the community? What real choice is offered by the national chains which tend to overwhelm effective local competition? What choice does an elderly rural resident have to buy services that will help him stay in his own home?
4. *Right to Be Heard*—This right, which is the right to be assured that full and sympathetic consideration be given to consumer interests in the formulation of government policy and fair and expeditious treatment in government's administrative tribunals, is not well developed. The greatest need is at the local level of government for consumer counsel to assist in redressing of wrongs. There is also need to develop representative consumer councils in rural communities to reflect the consumers' interests before public bodies.
5. *Right to Justice*—This has been added to the Kennedy four rights because of growing awareness of the need for better mechanisms

6. David P. Calvert and Marilyn S. Moody, *Help Yourself! A Handbook on Consumer Fraud,* Consumer Protection Div., Sedgwick County Courthouse, Wichita, Kans.

for obtaining justice and resolving conflicts. Systems that are economical and balanced are not available and are especially needed in rural communities. Specific areas worthy of attention are:

a. Establishment of a system of small claims courts to reduce the cost of obtaining justice or, alternatively, the development of arbitration boards and procedures for settling differences.

b. Establishment of inward WATS communication to county and state attorney general's offices to give the isolated resident access to sophisticated and reliable assistance.

c. Development of group legal counsel services to enable rural residents to become better informed about their legal rights and be less vulnerable to entrapment by contract.

Viable consumer education and protection programs that function effectively at the local-regional level of government must be developed. This would include studying the needs of consumers; reviewing prevailing ordinances, codes, and regulations and enforcement tools; and developing better mechanisms for effective consumer protection. Furthermore, consumer education must be considered as continuing education, not as education that can be terminated with school or entrusted entirely to commercial advertising. It is unreasonable for a college student to become sufficiently knowledgeable at that age about such matters as annuities and health insurance for the aged when these will not become relevant until decades later. All citizens should be entitled to objective education when it is appropriate and needed.

HOMEMAKER/HOME HEALTH AIDE SERVICE. The one recommendation that deserves unreserved endorsement as a priority mission-oriented, promotional, developmental research is the establishment of homemaker/home health programs so that the service is available to all citizens regardless of income, race, or age. It should be as available to the wealthy as to the poor; only the charge for service should vary.

1. There is a latent demand for this service with the result that the aged, the infirm, and the isolated are further disadvantaged. If their needs are being met, they are too often met at a higher cost by institutionalized care which takes the persons away from their homes.

2. A large potential supply of personnel is available in each rural community—women who have completed child bearing and whose household responsibilities are miminal. Most are not employed

and not even counted in the labor force because they "know" no jobs exist. However, with training at a cost of approximately $1,000 they can become employable in four weeks.[7] As workers they will gain in self-respect, be performing services for those who will appreciate their assistance, and be less dependent on their husbands and families or public welfare for support.

3. This constitutes a hometown industry that is 100 percent efficient in that it brings together two groups of people who can depend on each other and help each other; whatever money changes hands will stay in the community, and the lives of both groups will be benefited.

4. A predominant group of citizens in rural middle America greatly need this service. These are the aged, particularly those in need of health and transportation services. Too frequently all we offer the aged is isolation or institutional care. These are not in the best interest of those elderly who could stay at home if care were available. Nor is it best for the community; the cost of institutionalized care far exceeds the cost of homemaker service unless the situation requires constant and long-term care. It also reduces the capital costs requirement, since the elderly have their own homes and new facilities need not be constructed.

Homemaker/home health aide service may not save the world, but it will make people happier by enabling them to stay in their own homes. The marginal revenue from this venture will far exceed marginal cost.[8]

RESEARCH NEEDS. Priority must be given to identifying the needs and goals of those living in rural communities and improving systems for attaining them while at the same time preserving their dignity as consumers.

7. See Congressional Record—Senate 5482, Apr. 6, 1972.
8. See "Home Health Services," report to the Special Committee on Aging, U.S. Senate, Apr. 1972, esp. p. 64.

CHAPTER SEVEN

ECONOMIC RESEARCH PROBLEMS

WILBUR R. MAKI

DISCUSSION of economic development strategies is concerned with the formulation and implementation of a "long-run approach to the positive development of rural areas in the United States." Long-run development approaches are identified for achieving (1) balanced national growth in export-producing activities, (2) optimal management scale of service delivery, and (3) widespread citizen participation in social priority setting. Each of the development approaches has certain information requirements and knowledge needs [see 24 for discussion of research framework].

EXPORT BASE EXPANSION. Concern about lagging regions and rural-urban disparities is translated into domestic development strategies for enhancing the viability of an area's economic base. Early efforts in "rural industrialization" were motivated by the idea of creating new jobs where jobs were needed by inducing expanding or relocating industries to move into rural areas. Emphasis was on jobs and income as the primary and indeed only means of improving rural well-being [3, 4, 6, 15, 19, 20, 21].

By emphasizing the job-creating potentials of new industries, certain kinds of development approaches are favored—agricultural and industrial development, energy use and production, and public enterprise development—which are market-oriented approaches to the expansion of the export-producing activities. However, public enterprise development deals with the relaxation of supply constraints too. In addition land control, while primarily a state-level responsibility,

WILBUR R. MAKI is Professor of Agricultural and Applied Economics, University of Minnesota, St. Paul.

may involve both local and federal agencies in the development of statewide control measures for the purpose of promoting rural-urban balance. Hence public enterprise development and land control represent additional strategies for affecting the supply of resources in programs of balanced national development. The common element in each of the three sorts of strategies is the spatial economic scale of strategy design and implementation—not multicounty but multiarea, i.e., regional.

The Upper Midwest is used as a prototype development region to illustrate the results of disparities in the range of choice for business and households. Contrasting population trends occur for the core area (the seven-county Twin City metropolitan area) and the outlying areas. The core area is the first to be examined because it offers insight into the processes of regional change [see 23 for extended discussion and related tables and maps].

In 1950 the Minneapolis–St. Paul core area accounted for 22 percent of the total regional population; by 1970 the percentage had increased to 32. The core area growth of 55 percent for the 1950–70 period compares with the total growth of 3 percent for the rest of the region. The differential growth is associated with high levels of private investment in job-creating industrial and commercial activities in the core area.

An influence zone of approximately 100 miles around the core area includes the satellite cities of St. Cloud, Willmar, Mankato, Rochester, and Eau Claire. The third ring of satellite cities includes the subregional growth poles of approximately 100,000 people—Fargo-Moorhead, Sioux Falls, and Duluth-Superior. In addition Wausau, Wisconsin, which is within the second ring of satellite cities, is included. However, Wausau is dependent on Green Bay as well as Minneapolis–St. Paul, and Green Bay is part of the Chicago-Milwaukee regional system. Each of the second ring of satellite cities within a 100-mile influence zone has its own ring of satellite cities; these are the area service centers outside the regional core area zones of influence.

The regional center, the regional subcenters, and the dependent area centers form potential subregional development districts in the Upper Midwest. Where the big metropolitan regions have a common boundary, subregional development districts are likely to depend on both of the regional centers for certain high-order services, (e.g., Wausau–Green Bay subregional development district). Still other subregional development districts may be delineated in the big region focusing on the Minneapolis–St. Paul core area, but the identification of the core area of these districts is difficult because of their large geographic size and the lack of dependent satellite cities that might serve as subregional centers [9, 22, 30, 34].

One subregional center—Fargo-Moorhead—has been identified as a potential focal area for rural development programs in the Upper Midwest [1, 40]. Altogether seven environmental planning areas in western Minnesota and eastern North Dakota make up the multiarea district. In addition the Red River Basin segment of the Souris-Red-Rainy river basins planning region is included within the district boundaries [12].

Within the development district a fourteen-county environmental planning area has been selected for intensive study of the present and potential role of local government in subregional development. Seven so-called functional communities (i.e., local service areas) are delineated within the fourteen-county study area. Each of the functional communities is identified by a primary and a secondary area service center.

Area service centers have emerged in western Minnesota and elsewhere simply because of their dominant position in providing high-order services to smaller local centers and to the local open-country population. Together with the small local service centers, which often are county seat towns, the area centers have become the key links in an emerging decentralized system of state and federal services. To facilitate the trend toward economic decentralization, the regional development system must be established as a viable entity for achieving certain regional development objectives which are likely to be a part of national efforts in achieving balanced national growth [13, 30, 34, 36, 41].

Energy use and production are also involved in achieving balanced national growth. Regional energy requirements relate to national growth requirements. Projected energy requirements also are associated with given sets of assumptions about national environmental standards and use of pollution-reducing technologies and consumption-reducing pricing practices [19].

Subregional energy production depends only partly on subregional energy requirements. Because of new energy transfer systems, the location of energy production is a variable subject to environmental management constraints asserted at a subregional or area level of development planning. Hence the energy use and production subsystem in regional development will interact with environmental management considerations in regional conflict resolution, with the environmental impacts of energy production being specified for an entire planning area as well as particular points within the area.

Private entrepreneurship, including the provision of technical skills and financial support, becomes a critical development input for export-producing industries in the private sector [35, 37]. Private capital formation in the subregional producer/provider system, especially among small businesses, depends on the relaxation of supply constraints on output expansion. Hence public enterprise inputs, which would be represented by an appropriate mix of technical know-how, capital improvements, and manpower skills, are introduced as a means of achieving certain levels of regional development and growth because of the expansion of small business enterprises.

Public enterprise development is achieved through federal-state cooperation of the sort emerging under the Appalachian Regional Development Administration program [29]. Federal financing is coupled with state participation in the organization of local service delivery systems as well as in the planning and construction of economic and social infrastructure. The critical missing ingredient, however, has been flexibility in financing procedures, coupled with organizational and staffing limitations for assisting small businesses in expanding their marketing outlets and improving the efficiency of their plant operations.

Needed in the public entrepreneurship role is knowledge and information for projecting alternative regional futures based on alternative programs and projects for obtaining regional development goals. Also needed is an evaluative capability for assessing the probable impacts of the alternative programs and projects on specific segments of the area economy and population. In other words, a measure of the incidence of the benefits and costs of the proposed private investment and related public financing is being sought [4].

Land control is emerging as a central concern of the commissions and task forces recently established to study alternative population and growth policies for the United States [16]. Among state governments, concern over lakeshore land use, too rapid expansion of metropolitan peripheries, and the possibilities of establishing new towns and self-sustaining metropolitan centers is bringing up the issue of public control of land use and land values. Comprehensive state land-use planning would involve the full range of instruments of land control from outright purchase and ownership to alternative forms of leasing, retention of easements rights, taxation of capital gains, zoning, and subdivision control.

Congress is currently engaged in hearings on individual and corporate ownership of land in rural areas. Who owns rural America? In the metropolitan areas we are asking who owns the downtown, the diversified service centers in the outlying suburbs, and the open space now being held for purposes of speculative gains. Enveloped in the issue of ownership is the more decisive issue of control. Public control, however, can be asserted under private ownership.

Public control of land use and land value is exercised potentially at state and regional levels. Such control can be implemented at the multicounty level, but even at that level divergence of values among local interests in a region will divert land into uses that inevitably are conflicting and adverse to broad regional interests. Eventually the police powers heretofore confined almost totally to the municipal and county levels of government in zoning and subdivision controls may be pooled on a multicounty basis within an environmental planning area to sustain certain broad regional values in land use.

OPTIMAL MANAGEMENT SCALE OF SERVICE DELIVERY.

Unlike export base expansion, public service delivery is primarily an area management function of regional development. For purposes of this discussion, the area management function is confined to residuals recycling and disposal, public facility location, and capital budgeting. In addition, land control considerations are involved in area management of public services as well as in programs for achieving balanced national growth [11, 31, 39].

Each of the management concerns relates to decentralization of state government activities and improvement of consumer/user access to essential public services. Effective resolution of these management concerns is likely to require the existence of some form of multicounty councils of government for coordinating the public management activities on an areawide basis [14].

In residuals management the recycling and/or disposal of solid, liquid, gaseous, and thermal wastes are commonly included, along with abatement of noise and visual pollution. In many rural areas sewage disposal is a high-priority current local issue; in other areas conformance with new air quality standards or thermal pollution standards may be of primary concern. Altogether, control of the major forms of pollution—water, solid waste, and air—is estimated to cost $13.5 billion annually, of which a very small portion presumably will be incurred in rural areas [5].

Areawide control of sewage disposal has become a primary instrument of control of urban expansion into the countryside. Even roads and streets are less important than sewage hookup in controlling the conversion of agricultural areas into residential, commercial, and industrial land uses [10].

While sewer systems are being managed on an areawide scale in the multicounty Twin Cities metropolitan area, the appropriate systems management scale for sewage recycling and disposal in outstate Minnesota is much less extensive, covering only a few municipalities and townships. The small watershed probably is the appropriate management unit for rural and small-town sewage systems and less densely populated areas. Nonetheless, several small watersheds must cooperate on a multicounty scale to effectively control the pollution of a system of lakes for which the environmental planning function is undertaken on an areawide scale.

Public facility location—which includes the location of residuals management facilities as well as streets, roads, and highways—lacks the grass-roots participation that occurs in the residuals management issue area. Nevertheless, public facility location has its own partici- pant cluster from higher education, public schools, libraries, hospitals and health care facilities, parks and recreation areas, airports, streets, roads, highways, and fire and police stations. Within the general public, clientele groups emerge in potential area service centers that may be vying with one another to become a dominant center in a particular multicounty commuter shed. Policy on public facility lo- cations at the state level thus becomes a policy for regionalization of key governmental services, such as health care and education [10, 33, 38].

A facility systems model has been proposed which combines the original public (i.e. "noxious") facility to be located with a least-cost package of other (i.e. auxiliary) facilities and activities selected to minimize public cost at given risk levels [28]. In the short run such a model is viewed as a political placation model; in the long run it becomes a welfare distribution model in which long-run benefits and costs and their incidence among different groups in the impact area must be ascertained. Only the long-run approach, which takes into account specific gainers and losers in the facility location process and outcome, makes sense in terms of development strategy.

In rural areas the sharing of public facilities is widely accepted. A recent Minnesota poll shows that 70 percent of all adults support the idea of small towns joining together in regional groups to share schools, hospitals, and other facilities [26]. Those who favor regional sharing say that pooling resources provides more and better facilities at less cost. Those who think rural facility sharing is a poor idea say towns are too far apart and require too much travel. Many reasons— pro and con—are advanced on the issue of rural facility sharing, but the findings remain strongly supportive of the idea of merging a wide range of public facilities into one large service area and an area serv- ice center.

Capital budgeting, when undertaken on an areawide scale, must be accomplished concurrently with the public facility location. How- ever, areawide capital budgeting is a process that, if instituted, would work its way from the bottom up—from the many municipalities and townships in a multicounty area to the multicounty council of gov- ernment or its counterpart. Public facility location, on the other hand, works from the top down as a primary instrument of state and/ or federal regionalization policy. We expect much greater difficulties, therefore, in the implementation of areawide capital budgeting compared with a statewide policy of public facility location [2, 8, 16].

Presently the multicounty councils of government in the United States are primarily clearing houses rather than areawide coordinating agencies for capital improvement programs [27]. However, legal and legislative bases exist in several states for areawide coordination of capital improvements to be effective, provided the areawide body is willing to require review of special-purpose district and municipal programs and budgets at one time so that budgeting priorities can be established not within a single special-purpose function but between functions.

An optimal management scale for service delivery involves some considering of land control. Land control is a municipal, township, or county government function when exercised in the form of zoning or subdivision control. Differential taxation of agricultural lands or taxation of development gains is typically a state government function. Outright fee simple purchase of private lands by any governmental or quasi-governmental agency may or may not require prior exercise of the right of eminent domain. Alternatively, a limited property right, through an easement purchase or a leaseback arrangement, may be acquired by a local or state government agency. Thus a wide array of policy instruments for limited land control is available, but not necessarily for an areawide resource management agency [10, 31].

CITIZEN PARTICIPATION IN SOCIAL PRIORITY SETTING.

Of the three "cutting edges" of regional rural-urban development, social priority setting may be the sharpest, but it presents a deeply troublesome dilemma. To what extent and for whom is any loss in local autonomy compensated by the gains in economy and access as a result of larger management systems for producing and providing essential social services?

Technical modeling capabilities provide only partial answers to the fundamental dilemma. We are trying to establish the data base and the criteria for determining the economies of scale in service delivery, but we lack the noneconomic criteria for determining the noneconomic or nonmonetized costs of larger service delivery systems [32].

Even more serious is our inability to establish priorities between program areas—e.g., roads vs. schools. Disagreement over goals and values, however, becomes confused with data problems and communication difficulties. More sophisticated information and communications systems are being developed, but we continue to disagree even more strongly than before because of fundamental conflicts—

implicitly if not explicitly—in goals and values [7, 17, 18, 25]. Therefore, social priority setting is viewed as a three-fold task: (1) identifying and delineating broad goal areas sought by citizens of a region; (2) relating the goal areas to program areas which are ranked in terms of their perceived or expected contribution to their respective goal areas and thus to the quality of life in the region; and (3) seeking program area agreement on specific projects that best meet given program area objectives.

REFERENCES

1. Angus, James, *Spatial Distribution of Employment: Alternatives for a Metropolitan Region,* unpublished Ph.D. thesis, Univ. Minn., 1973.
2. Barnard, Jerald R., *Design and Use of Social Accounting Systems in State Development Planning,* Bureau of Business and Economic Research, Univ. Iowa, 1967.
3. Barnard, Jerald R., James A. Macmillan, and Wilbur R. Maki, "Evaluation models for regional development planning," *Papers Regional Science Association,* 23:117–38, 1969.
4. Beckman, Norman, "Development of national urban growth policy," *J. Amer. Inst. Planners,* 37(3):146–61, 1971.
5. *Business Week,* "The annual cost of pollution control" (based on Harvard Center for Population Studies data), Jan. 3, 1970, p. 64.
6. Cameron, Gordon C., *Regional Economic Development: The Federal Role* (Baltimore and London: Johns Hopkins Press, 1970).
7. Center for Real Estate and Urban Economics, *Jobs, People and Land: Bay Area Simulation Study (BASS),* Univ. Calif., Institute of Urban and Regional Development, 1968.
8. Crecine, John P., *Governmental Problem Solving: A Computer Simulation of Municipal Budgeting,* American Politics Research Series (Chicago: Rand McNally, 1969).
9. Downs, Anthony, "Alternative forms of future urban growth in the United States," *J. Amer. Inst. Planners,* 36(1):3–11, 1970.
10. Friedan, Bernard J., *Metropolitan America: Challenge to Federalism,* Advisory Commission on Intergovernmental Relations, M-31, Washington, D.C., 1966.
11. Gabler, L. R., "Economies and Diseconomies of Scale in Urban Public Sectors," *Land Economics,* 45(4):425–34, 1969.
12. Hamilton, H. R., et al., *Systems Simulation for Regional Analysis, An Application to River-Basin Planning* (Cambridge, Mass.: MIT Press, 1969).
13. Hansen, Niles, *Intermediate Size Cities as Growth Centers: Applications for Kentucky, the Piedmont Crescent, the Ozarks and Texas* (New York: Praeger Publishers, 1971).
14. Hanson, Royce, *Metropolitan Councils of Government,* Advisory Commission on Intergovernmental Relations, M-32, Washington, D.C., 1966.
15. Harris, C. C., Jr., and M. C. McGuire, "Planning Techniques for Regional Development Policy," *J. Human Resources,* Vol. 4, No. 4, Fall 1969.
16. Haskell, Elizabeth, "New directions in state environmental planning," *J. Amer. Inst. Planners,* 37(4):253–57, 1971.

17. Isard, Walter, and Thyrias W. Langford, *Regional Input-Output Study: Recollections, Reflections and Diverse Notes on the Philadelphia Experience* (Cambridge: MIT Press, 1971).

18. Isard, Walter, et al., *Ecological-Economic Analysis for Regional Development* (New York: Free Press, 1972).

19. Leven, Charles L., John B. Legler, and Perry Shapiro. *An analytical framework for regional development policy,* Regional Science Study No. 9 (London and Cambridge, Mass.: MIT Press, 1970).

20. Macmillan, J. A., "Regional Development Planning Theory and Practice," *Perspectives in Regional Economics,* Vol. IV, 1973.

21. Maki, Wilbur R., Richard E. Suttor, and Jerald R. Barnard. *Simulation of Regional Product and Income with Emphasis on Iowa, 1954–1974,* Iowa Agr. and Home Econ. Exp. Sta. Res. Bull. 548, 1966. See also: Maki, Wilbur R., Jerald R. Barnard, and Richard E. Suttor, "Recursive economic systems in rural-urban development," *J. Farm Econ.,* 46:466–74, 1964.

22. Maki, Wilbur R., "Infrastructure in rural areas," in *Rural Poverty in the United States,* President's National Advisory Commission on Rural Poverty (Washington, D.C.: GPO, 1968), pp. 86–109.

23. Maki, Wilbur R., and Ernesto Venegas, "The emptying of the countryside and its cost," in *Symposium on the Labor Force: Migration, Earnings and Growth,* TVA and SSA, Muscle Shoals, Ala., 1973.

24. Maki, Wilbur R., "Social/environmental systems for regional development planning," *Regional Science Perspectives,* Vol. 4, 1973.

25. Miernyk, William H., et al., *Simulating Regional Economic Development: An Interindustry Analysis of the West Virginia Economy* (Lexington, Mass.: D. C. Heath, 1970).

26. *Minneapolis Tribune,* "Minnesota poll: 70% back rural facilities sharing," Aug. 11, 1968.

27. Mogulog, Melvin B., "Regional planning, clearance, and evaluation: A look at the A-95 process," *J. Amer. Inst. Planners,* 37(6):418–21, 1971.

28. Mumphrey, Anthony J., Jr., John E. Seley, and Julian Wolpert, "A decision model for locating controversial facilities," *J. Amer. Inst. Planners,* 37(6):397–402, 1971.

29. National Area Development Institute, *Area Development Interchange,* Vol. II, No. 1, Jan. 1, 1972.

30. Neutze, G. M., *Economic Policy and the Size of Cities* (Canberra: Australian National Univ., 1965).

31. Ostrom, V., "Operational Federalism: Organization for the Provision of Public Services in the American Federal System," *Public Choice,* Vol. 6, Spring 1969.

32. Pavelis, George A., *Planning National Resource Development: An Introductory Guide,* Agr. Handbook 431, USDA, 1972.

33. Schultz, G. P., "Facility Planning for a Public Service System: Domestic Solid Waste Collection," *J. Regional Science,* 9(2):291–307, 1969.

34. Shacker, Arie S., "Israel's development towns: evaluation of national urbanization policy," *J. Amer. Inst. Planners,* 37(6):362–72, 1971.

35. Shane, Mathew, *The Flow of Funds Through the Commerical Banking System, Minnesota-North Dakota,* Minn. Agr. Exp. Sta. Bull. 506, 1972.

36. Sundquist, James L., *Making Federalism Work* (Washington, D.C.: Brookings Institution, 1969).

37. Thompson, Wilbur R., *A Preface to Urban Economics* (Baltimore: Johns Hopkins Press, 1965).

38. Tietz, Michael B., "Towards a theory of urban public facility location," *Papers Regional Science Association,* 21:35–51, 1968.
39. Tullock. G., "Federalism: Problems of Scale," *Public Choice,* Vol. 6, Spring 1969.
40. Ulrich, Martin A., and Wilbur R. Maki, *Financing Public Services in West Minnesota.* Minn. Agr. Exp. Sta. Bull. 509, 1973.
41. U.S. Department of Commerce, *Area Redevelopment Policies in Britain and the Countries of the Common Market,* Economic Redevelopment Administration, 1965.

CHAPTER EIGHT

SOCIOLOGICAL RESEARCH PROBLEMS

OLAF F. LARSON

TO PROVIDE GUIDELINES for a judgment as to sociological research problems for rural development, it is important to establish the criteria for research priorities or at least suggest a framework for getting at the priorities. This is an essential but neglected exercise. One approach is to start with a concept of rural development, indicate the elements involved in the concept, and then see what central questions based on some theoretical framework are raised.

For a start and for our present purposes, let us take the statement: "A basic dimension underlying most definitions of development is that of a futuristic view; certain goals or consequences are valued, and social modifications are initiated to achieve these goals. . . . This future orientation suggests the difference between change and development."[1] Further, from a sociological point of view, development "may be seen as the identification of goals, the planning of strategies, and the modification of social structures so as to increase a social system's goal-attainment ability."[2] Let us assume that the scope of rural development encompasses such areas as economic development, community facilities, human resource development, and environmental quality. "Rural" for development purposes will be operationally defined to refer to low-density areas and smaller communities, excluding at the upper limit census-defined "urbanized

OLAF F. LARSON is Professor of Rural Sociology, New York State College of Agriculture and Life Sciences, Cornell University, and Director, Northeast Regional Center for Rural Development.

1. George M. Beal, Ronald C. Powers, and E. Walter Coward (eds.), *Sociological Perspectives of Domestic Development* (Ames: Iowa State Univ. Press, 1971), pp. 265–66.
2. Ibid., p. 266.

areas"—i.e., places of 50,000 population or more and their immediate densely settled environs. Coupling this conception with the clues from the location-specific practitioner and the broad national-level perspective could lead to a translation and interpretation something like the following:

Two general categories of social units are, for analytical purposes, involved in rural development: (1) individuals and (2) collections or groups to which we can give the general title "social system" and under which we can subsume all the special cases—economic, educational, delivery of health services, etc. The system-type units are linked to and built upon the individual-type units. These social systems (more correctly, subsystems) may be the targets for change by rural development policies and programs; they are the means, the instruments, through which rural development is carried out. Rural sociologists have made so much use of the social system model, especially the framework offered by Loomis, that detailed explanation seems unnecessary.[3] It may suffice to say that the Loomis model includes the "conditions of social action"—that is, the setting of the system in space and in time, together with the size of the system.[4] A system may be characterized as having a structure. It includes analytically identifiable parts (elements) internal to the system, such as beliefs, goals, and norms. It includes analytically identifiable processes within the system such as decision making and evaluation. Among the "master processes" are those which bear on the relationship among systems, such as linkage and boundary maintenance. Since systems vary widely in size, territorial limits, and complexity, one might think of them broadly in micro, macro, and intermediate terms.

If rural development is future-oriented, if it operates through social systems, what are the crucial questions within the system framework about which we have sociological knowledge that can be put to use? What are the questions on which more research is needed?

3. The most complete statement of Loomis's conceptual scheme may be found in Charles P. Loomis, *Social Systems: Essays on Their Persistence and Change* (Princeton, N.J.: D. Van Nostrand Co., 1960), pp. 1–40. The use of this social system model in analysis related to rural development is illustrated by Ronald C. Powers, "Sociological strategies in a multicounty development program: A case in sociologing," in Beal, Powers, and Coward. See also Ronald C. Powers, "Multicounty units as a basis for domestic change programs," in Luther T. Wallace, Daryl Hobbs, and Raymond D. Vlasin (eds.), *Selected Perspectives for Community Resource Development* (Raleigh, N.C.: Agricultural Policy Institute, N.C. State Univ., 1969). The Loomis model is reproduced in Powers's "Sociological strategies" article.

4. My view is that the theoretical basis for rural-urban differentiation rests in the conditions of social action represented by density and size of population aggregates. See Olaf F. Larson, "The Meaning of Rural," Dept. Rural Sociology, Cornell Univ.

PRIORITIES FOR SOCIOLOGICAL RESEARCH. The most crucial sociological questions for rural development have to do with
the following broad areas.[5]

1. Goals
2. Strategies for achieving goals
   a. Determination of exogenous variables of the "input" type
      instrumental for intervention
   b. Determination of systems and variables within the system
      of the organizational and process type
3. Evaluation of policies and programs pertaining to rural development
4. Analysis of the basic current situation and social trends in
   America and of the "limiting conditions" in the rural setting

Existing sociological research is limited in what it can now offer
in the area of goals and in what it can now provide with respect to
exogenous instrumental variables. It has more to offer in the area
of organizational and process strategies and probably more concerning
"limiting conditions." However, the existing research-based knowledge is not widely known, and what we do "know" is not always used
or may be used ineffectively in rural development policy formulation
and in program planning.

Need for Synthesis. The need is urgent to give greater attention to
the retrieval, synthesis, and interpretation for rural development
purposes of the sociological research already accumulated. Some
of this research-based knowledge is in professional journals that
have escaped attention. Some is in the fugitive literature—mimeo-
graphed publications that did not get in the libraries, preliminary
reports given limited circulation and never carried to the final version. The task may include reanalysis of data already in the files to
gain new insights with new analytical tools, to test hypotheses derived
from new conceptual approaches. Such efforts may not always be
exciting if judged by conventional norms of researchers, but the
payoff in the interest of rural development might be high for the
resources invested.

What, for example, would a critical review of the accumulated
research suggest about alternative systems of health care delivery for

5. The specific questions and the weighting of their relative importance may
   be influenced not only by the conception one has of the nature and scope
   of rural development but also by the theoretical orientation as to planned
   change which is accepted. Hobbs, pointing out that there is no single
   sociological theory of change, selected for review four theoretical approaches to which he gave the broad labels "functionalism, modernization,
   conflict, and social behaviorism"; Daryl J. Hobbs, "Some contemporary
   sociological perspectives regarding social change," in Beal, Powers, and
   Coward.

rural people? What is known about the interrelation of the distribution of different types of health facilities and their use? At what point or under what circumstances does distance make a difference in use? Would the available evidence support the desire of small communities to have a doctor? What is the relationship between mortality and sickness among the people of a community and alternative patterns of access to health and medical care facilities?

What does the research we now have tell us about what happens when specific subsystems are merged to serve a larger territory? What happens to voluntary participation, to locality group identification, to community solidarity? What is lost, what is gained, what substitutes arise when the territorial base of operations is enlarged? The past research on public school centralization[6] and what happened when open-country rural churches gave way to village-located churches[7] might have some relevance for the increasing emphasis on multicounty organization.

To what extent is there support for the implications drawn from a study of one small rural community in the Northeast which gives the social importance of neighborhood groups a new interpretation for today's society, suggesting that they may be the only real means of relating many rural people to the larger society?[8] Their absence or the failure to tie them to larger social structures may lead to alienation of the local residents. The costs of ignoring them in the name of efficiency and rationality may be high and may subvert the intent of centralization, and we may find hopeful efforts to solve rural problems achieving little more than paper empires.

Voluntary associations abound in many rural communities. What can we glean from available research as to the role of such organizations as community change agents and as resolvers of community issues? Is there evidence that those associations which most frequently introduce changes for the community as a whole have predictable characteristics?[9]

6. See, for example, Eugene T. Stromberg, *The Influence of the Central Rural School on Community Organization,* Cornell Univ. Agr. Exp. Sta. Bull. 699, 1938.
7. Edmund deS. Brunner and J. H. Kolb, *Rural Social Trends* (New York: McGraw-Hill Book Co., 1933), p. 210; Theodore C. Scheifele and William G. Mather, *Closed Rural Pennsylvania Churches* (Pa. Agr. Exp. Sta., 1949) cited by John H. Kolb and Edmund deS. Brunner, *A Study of Rural Society,* 4th ed. (Boston, Mass.: Houghton Mifflin Company, 1952), p. 363.
8. Ruth C. Young and Olaf F. Larson, "The social ecology of a rural community," *Rural Sociology,* 35:337–53, 1970.
9. One study, for example, found that high-prestige associations were more likely than those of medium or low prestige to introduce changes for the community as a whole. High-prestige associations originated relations with other community organizations more frequently; they tended to be longer established, have more members, and be more closely identified with the main institutions of the community. See Ruth C. Young and Olaf F. Larson, "The contribution of voluntary organizations to community structure," *Amer. J. Sociol.,* 71:178–86, 1965.

From scrutiny of past experiences with development can we identify principles that, if followed, increase the likelihood of successful linkage between planning and action, of linkage between elected officials and representative citizen groups, of linkage between community and state and federal agencies, and of program continuity?[10] What do we already know about strategies that work most effectively in involving the more disadvantaged members of a community in problem identification, goal determination, and program formation?[11]

In view of the commitment made by Congress in the Agriculture Act of 1970 "to a sound balance between rural and urban America," in view of recommendations that point toward a national policy of a more widely dispersed population (such as was made by the President's Task Force on Rural Development), and in the light of the magnitude of the mobility of the nation's people between rural and urban areas, what can we learn from available research about people's preferences as to residential patterns and weighting of different factors in the movement of people to and from dispersed and concentrated settlement?

Studies of "Limiting Conditions" and of Trends. Research on the current situation and major social trends in rural America and on the "limiting conditions" in the rural setting should be a major component of any basic and continuing research program concerned with rural life. Such research, properly done, is necessary to provide an understanding of American rural society as it is today and clues as to future directions. The results of such research might give us an early alert to emerging problems. They could help clarify rural development issues, the choice of goals, and the selection of development strategies.

Other than the excellent demographic work made possible by census data and illustrated by the work of Calvin Beale and his associates, we probably know less about American rural society today than we knew about our nation's rural life in the 1920s, 1930s, and 1940s.[12] We need to give more attention to the consequences of the

10. Strengths and weaknesses of one experimental approach to development at the community level are summarized in Olaf F. Larson, "Some Extension Experiences in Community Development," paper presented at Conference on Rural Development for Cooperative Extension Service in Northeastern Region, New York City, Mar. 7–8, 1961 (mimeo.).

11. For reports on early innovative efforts to help low-income farm families, see Rachel Rowe and Olaf F. Larson, *A Ten-County Program Experiment with 606 Low-Income Rural Families*, Dept. Rural Sociology Bull. 68, Cornell Univ., 1966; and Olaf F. Larson, *Ten Years of Rural Rehabilitation in the United States*, Bur. Agr. Econ., USDA, 1947.

12. In the 1920s and 1930s we had the benefit of the repeated studies in a nationwide sample of village-centered communities initiated by Edmund deS. Brunner. See Edmund deS. Brunner, Gwendolyn S. Hughes, and Marjorie Patten, *American Agricultural Villages* (New York: Doran and

basic factors that underlie rural-urban differentation and to the public policy implications of these underlying factors. Three lines of research need continuing attention:

1. If it is correct that the basic factor underlying rural-urban differentiation has to do with the distribution of people in space—i.e., size of place and density ("conditions of social action" in the social system framework)—in what ways do size and density make a difference in social systems, in social and economic organization, and ultimately in the well-being of people?[13] What are the means of overcoming any adverse effects of given conditions of size/density, be it low density or large size, on those aspects of systems that bear on the goal achievements of people? What are the costs of modifying such adverse effects?

2. In a period of such rapid change the need is especially great for a constant updating of the information base about trends and the current situation. We need to know in a more comprehensive and representative way what is happening to the social systems in American rural society—somewhat as we have knowledge of the number, distribution, migration, and composition of the population. This leads to studies of social change and to special consideration from a public policy perspective of what is being referred to as social indicators.

Since the mid-1960s there has been growing attention to social indicators.[14] From the viewpoint of rural development information requirements, particular attention needs to be given to criterion variables in order to avoid using scarce resources in dragnet data-collecting and statistical operations.

Land stresses that economic statistics that are labeled economic indicators are so designated primarily because of their nexus in

Company, 1927); Edmund deS. Brunner and J. H. Kolb, *Rural Social Trends* (New York: McGraw-Hill, 1933); Edmund deS. Brunner and Irving Lorge, *Rural Trends in Depression Years* (New York: Columbia Univ. Press, 1937). In the 1940s the series of studies organized by the Bureau of Agricultural Economics, USDA, in a set of counties distributed among major type-of-farming areas had the potential to provide a national and regional overview, had it been continued with time series and depth studies as originally envisaged; results of initial reconnaissance work were summarized in Chs. 19–27 of Carl C. Taylor et al., *Rural Life in the United States* (New York: Alfred A. Knopf, 1949).

13. See Larson, "The Meaning of Rural." Recent empirical work which deals on a county unit basis with the general problem raised here is represented by Herman Bluestone, *Focus for Area Development Analysis: Urban Orientation of Counties*, Agr. Econ. Rept. 183, USDA, ERS, 1970; analyses on a multicounty basis are represented by Clark Edwards, Robert Coltrane, and Stan Daberkow, *Regional Variations in Economic Growth and Development with Emphasis on Rural Areas*, Agr. Econ. Rept. 205, USDA, ERS, 1971.

14. George M. Beal et al., *Social Indicators: Bibliography I*, Sociology Rept. 92, Dept. Sociol. and Anthropol., Iowa State Univ., 1971.

some model of the economy; they are indicators because they tell something about the functioning of the economy. He would propose a similar criterion for defining social indicators, using the term to comprise those social statistics that (a) "are components in a sociological . . . model of a social system or some particular segment or process thereof," (b) "can be collected at a sequence of points in time and accumulated into a time-series," and (c) "can be aggregated or disaggregated to levels appropriate to the specifications of the model."[15] Granting the major unsolved problems in social indicators, Land calls for macrosociological models of what we have termed education, health, and welfare and corresponding systems and their processes. Given such models, analysis would be needed to establish the sensitivity of output variables to input variables, thus providing knowledge that could facilitate policy decisions at the macro level with respect to specific systems.

3. From the standpoint of information needs for rural development national policy and program purposes, information on rural society aggregated to the national level is not sufficient. The figures for rural-urban population trends do not apply universally. For example, in contrast to recent national trends, in New York (which now ranks third in size of census-defined rural population) the number rural is now the largest recorded, and the rural-urban balance has changed little in forty years. What are the important variations in the underlying conditions within the rural sector of the nation, the variations in systems and system characteristics, and the variations in rates and direction of change of both underlying conditions and systems? For example, a simple Guttman-type scale can be used to demonstrate the variations among states in their rural-urban experience over more than a century. Two states have experienced 120 years of urban dominance; a few states continue to be predominantly rural. The rural population density among states in 1960 varied more than fiftyfold. An indication of variations among states in the social class of the farm population is given in a recent article.[16] What would the results be if extended to the total rural population, farm and nonfarm? To what extent are rising income levels reflected in shifts among states in their comparative positions, or in narrowing the spread among states in per capita income, or in a convergence of income distribution patterns among the states?[17] In which systems, for which characteris-

---

15. Kenneth C. Land, *Social Indicators* (Russell Sage Foundation, 1970), p. 39 (mimeo.).
16. T. Lynn Smith, "A study of social stratification in the agricultural sections of the U.S.: Nature, data, procedures, and preliminary results," *Rural Sociology*, 34:498–509, 1969.
17. Although per capita personal income has increased in all states over the last half-century and there has been a tendency to reduce the spread

tics, and in which geographic areas does change readily occur? In which does change occur slowly? Is there an identifiable sequence in the changes that occur? A comparative approach, in space as well as in time, is necessary to provide some of the basic information about our society in a nation so extensive in geography and so diverse in background and development history.

Goals. If development is conceptualized as goal-oriented change, the choice of goals becomes crucial for policy and program purposes.

The goals of rural development are set in the context of goals for the nation as a whole. The interplay of goals of the complex set of systems within and among the different territorial levels may lead to dilemmas. Costs and benefits of given policies are unlikely to be distributed equally among individuals or areas. The relevance of conceptually defining goals and of specifying empirical measures is suggested by the hypothesis that intangible goals result in goal displacement and low goal attainment.[18]

Among the questions which may be raised concerning rural development goals from the perspective of rural America are these:

1. What is the range of alternative goals for rural development, and what weights or priorities are attached to these alternatives by decision makers? By rural people? By different categories of rural people? The President's Task Force on Rural Development called for guiding policies in the framework of the total economic and social development of the nation in such areas as population distribution, industrial dispersion, land use, resource management, food and fiber production, rural housing, educational programs, employment, national growth, and quality of life.[19] A comparable set of policy issues was identified in the context of the development of a national growth policy by the National Goals Research staff.[20] Thomas Nagel, a philosopher, contends that the latter report is not fundamental enough, that it assumes that a general set of goals for the nation is defined by an increase in the avail-

between the high and low state in per capita income, the positions of states relative to each other has shown a high degree of stability, especially among the lower-income states. See Frank A. Hanna, *State Income Differentials, 1919–1954* (Durham, N.C.: Duke Univ. Press, 1959), pp. 38–41; Advisory Commission on Intergovernmental Relations, *Measuring the Fiscal Capacity and Effort of State and Local Areas* (Washington, D.C.: GPO, 1971), pp. 120–21.

18. Beal, Powers, and Coward, p. 266.
19. U.S. President's Task Force on Rural Development, *A New Life for the Country* (Washington, D.C.: GPO, 1970), p. 11.
20. National Goals Research Staff, *Toward Balanced Growth: Quantity with Quality* (Washington, D.C.: GPO, 1970).

ability of certain generally accepted goods and a reduction of certain generally accepted evils.[21]

How would such rural development objectives as the following be rated in relation to the more conventional economic criteria or broad goals of rural-urban balance or better population distribution: more equitable distribution of income, reduction of alienation, preservation of cultural integrity and cultural and social diversity, and increasing the number and representativeness of those involved in the decision-making process with respect to goal determination?

2. What values held by rural people underlie and influence their choice of development goals? What values serve as guides in the policy-making process or for given policy areas? Nagel, for example, identifies paternalism, elitism, and distributive justice as alternative approaches to deciding what is desirable as a national policy in the interest of individual members of a society.[22] The study of values, especially values specific to rural people, has been a neglected area of research. The few nationwide studies that purport to bear upon rural-urban differences in values merely compare farmers with other occupational groups.[23]

3. What are the processes by which goals of development are determined? What is the interrelationship of goal setting among the several systems and system levels? On the more local level, to what extent are goals externally imposed rather than the result of an interaction process within the locality? Who is involved in goal determination? What is the interplay between the public and private sectors?

Strategies. The achievement of rural development ends is influenced by the "limiting conditions" in the rural setting which serve as constraints, by other variables not subject to control by the policy maker, and by the means or policy instruments used. The policy instruments are (1) the exogenous "input" variables and (2) systems, with their internal organizational variables and processes.

With respect to input variables, research is needed to determine the relationship, for given systems and under specified conditions, of inputs to outputs—i.e., to goal achievement. It is necessary to determine whether inputs have the expected effect, directly or indirectly, on desired results.

21. Thomas Nagel, "Reason and national goals," *Science,* 177:766–70, 1972.
22. Ibid.
23. Howard W. Beers, "Rural-urban differences: Some evidence from public opinion polls," *Rural Sociology,* 18:1–11, 1953; Norval D. Glenn and Jon P. Alston, "Rural-urban differences in reported attitudes and behavior," *Southwestern Social Science Quarterly,* 47:381–400, 1967.

Work by Stewart on the relation of measures of types of health systems—i.e., treatment, prevention, and information—to life expectancy is illustrative of the kind of assumptions that need to be questioned. Using all nations in the Western Hemisphere plus Puerto Rico as units of analysis, he found no significant relationship between number of doctors per 10,000 population or number of hospital beds per 1,000 population (treatment measures) and life expectancy, the dependent variable.[24] In contrast, the measure of prevention (percent of population supplied with potable water) and the measure of information (literacy rate was used as a surrogate) were significantly related to life expectancy. For the United States Stewart's data show marked changes in mortality and life expectancy over the period 1900–1960 not matched by ratios of medical personnel and hospital facilities to population. The findings raise issues concerning the allocation of resources among types of health systems and possibly between health and other systems.

Sharkansky examined the relationship between levels of state and local spending and measures of public service quantity or quality in six fields (such as education, health and hospitals, and public safety) using simple and partial correlation analysis. He found "that gross levels of spending do not reflect service levels, and that gross increases in spending are not likely to produce early gross improvements in services."[25]

Of 204 possible relationships between spending and services, only 78 were found to be significant by simple correlation; but 37 were not in the expected direction. The relationships were even weaker under partial correlation. In an analysis of the school districts of one state, Sharkansky found a weak relationship between a set of eight policy (input) measures and his measures of educational output.[26] He also noted a disparity between the results of macro- and micro-analyses with the same variables in the area of education.

Such findings reemphasize the need for analysis to establish the sensitivity of input to output variables. They lend support to the argument that expenditures, as inputs, are related to output variables through the organization of the particular system under study.[27] Also, aggregated measures of output (as in the case of health or education at state and national levels) are the results of the operation of many concrete systems, not the result of a single firm.

24. Charles T. Stewart, Jr., "Allocation of resources to health," *J. Human Resources,* 6 (1):103–22, 1971.
25. Ira Sharkansky, "Government expenditures and public services in the American states," in Ira Sharkansky (ed.), *Policy Analysis in Political Science* (Chicago: Markham Publishing Company, 1970), p. 19.
26. Ira Sharkansky, "Environment, policy, output and impact: Problems of theory and method in the analysis of public policy," in Sharkansky (ed.)
27. Land, p. 59.

We note a multiplication of many types of systems (public, private, or mixed) for many purposes related to development—e.g., voluntary associations, community action agencies as a part of the OEO program, rural development committees, and multicounty organizations for planning. Since systems may be interpreted as means for achieving designated goals, one may ask whether research can contribute to devising alternative forms of organization for more effective goal achievement. For example, can research evidence suggest alternative systems for the delivery of health services to people in low-density areas, giving consideration to type of service and degree of specialization or to linkage of supporting services? Along with the best size of system for a particular function to achieve economies of scale, can research assist in determining the best fit of system as judged perhaps by such indicators as participation, alienation, and satisfaction?

Can the work on the structural characteristics of communities, using scalogram analysis, be used to aid in making decisions as to where and when to locate certain social and economic services with the greatest likelihood of success? A recent study in which facilities, programs, and services in 144 communities were inventoried would suggest that some communities, in terms of a sequential process of development, were "ready" for facilities they were lacking; others were "ahead of their time."[28] Longitudinal research could determine the success or failure of planned intervention in accord with or in defiance of the readiness of communities as judged by their scale position. This may offer a counter approach to conventional growth center strategy.

In view of the importance that planning has for all systems concerned with rural development and considering the growth of specialized planning agencies whose work has implications for rural development, research on the planning process and study of planning organizations deserves consideration. What information base is accessible to local planning units and used as a basis for planning and decision making? What organizational forms and procedures are instrumental in arriving at decisions and in translating decisions into action? What is the intersystem exchange, what are the linkages, and what is the boundary maintenance among systems planning for a common geographic territory or dealing with a common problem or related problems?

Evaluation. Baker identified 494 programs in 41 different federal departments and agencies that offered some type of financial or technical aid to localities outside heavily urbanized sections.[29] It

28. Philip Taietz, *Community Structure and Aging* (Ithaca, N.Y.: Dept. Rural Sociology, Cornell Univ., 1970).
29. U.S. Congress, Senate, Committee on Agriculture and Forestry, *Guide to Federal Programs for Rural Development,* by John A. Baker, S. Doc. 92-54, 92d Cong., 1st Sess. (2nd ed.; Washington, D.C.: GPO, 1971).

is little wonder that the President's Task Force on Rural Development reported itself stymied in carrying out its charge to evaluate how present federally supported rural development programs are working.[30]

Effective evaluation research is required in order to compare the consequences of a program—the actual goal achievement—with what was intended and to seek an explanation for discrepancies between plan and performance. Such research has its own requirements and special problems.[31] Although controlled experimental situations are typically difficult to incorporate in action program design or to maintain,[32] a multitude of natural experiments is going on all the time, study of which should strengthen our knowledge base about rural development strategies. A comprehensive approach to evaluation not only would include evaluation of ongoing programs but would endeavor to provide some assessment of such large questions as rural-urban population balance and population dispersion and concentration. It would give attention to specific development strategies such as the "growth center" concept[33] and to rural industrialization.

The greatest payoff for rural development in the long run may come from devoting research resources to the macro and intermediate level problems as against dispersing these resources on micro location-specific problems. A high priority should be assigned to systematically synthesizing for rural development purposes the research knowledge already accumulated so as to provide a sociological perspective for the policy decisions and program implementation which will not wait for the results of new long-run research.

30. U.S. President's Task Force on Rural Development, p. 13.
31. Daryl Hobbs, "Evaluation of area resource development programs," in Wallace, Hobbs, and Vlasin. It might be noted that a Committee on Federal Agency Evaluation Research has been set up by the Behavioral Sciences Division in the National Research Council of the National Academy of Sciences.
32. See Peter H. Rossi, "Practice, method, and theory in evaluating social-action programs," in James L. Sundquist (ed.) On Fighting Poverty: Perspectives from Experience, Vol. 2 (New York: Basic Books, 1969).
33. The need to define the appropriate role of growth centers in area development is stated by Alan R. Bird in "Needs and Potential for Research in Rural Development," paper presented at annual meeting of the Western Agricultural Economics Association, Squaw Valley, Calif., July 27, 1971.

CHAPTER NINE

RESEARCH RESOURCES FOR
MICROPOLITAN DEVELOPMENT

LUTHER TWEETEN

RESEARCH ON RURAL economic development has been fragmented, nonadditive, and overly positivistic. It has focused too often on "what is" rather than on "what could be" or "what ought to be." More importantly it has lacked a unifying framework to focus research resources on essential issues. This chapter contains normative judgments as well as a normative framework for research. The term *normative* as used herein is generally conditional, specifying that *if* the norm is development, *then* certain conclusions follow.

DEFINING MICROPOLITAN DEVELOPMENT. Issues addressed here often are researched under terms such as area, regional, community, rural, or resource development. Some delimitation of effort is warranted, since our research does not deal directly with the metropolis and its problems of the ghetto, violence, congestion, air pollution, and central city decay. The term "rural development" to describe our efforts is too restrictive—rural has become associated with open country and towns of 2,500 or less population as defined by the U.S. Census. While it is essential to include larger cities in our analysis, the term "nonmetropolitan" is too cumbersome. I propose the term *micropolitan development* to delimit our research and define the term as an increase in the well-being of people in micropolis, wherever they eventually reside.

LUTHER TWEETEN is Regents Professor, Department of Agricultural Economics, Oklahoma State University, Stillwater.

APPROACHES TO MICROPOLITAN DEVELOPMENT. In the past, two general approaches to micropolitan economic development have been considered—bringing people to jobs and bringing jobs to people. Looking at development efforts in the past decade, neither of these has been emphasized in the research and action programs of the USDA or the land-grant institutions. A third approach is transfer payments—compensation to losers from the development process (including school districts that finance approximately half the cost of educating micropolitan residents and see much of their investment lost through net spillouts to other areas) and public assistance to persons with low incomes who cannot earn a socially acceptable income. The fourth general approach to development is community organization and action to bring a more nearly optimal community resource combination.

Community Resource Development. Community resource development is defined in the Extension Committee on Organization and Policy (ECOP) report [5] and by community development specialists as "a *process* whereby those in a community arrive at group decisions and take actions to enhance the social and economic welfare and well-being of the community." There are some problems with this definition.

First, the emphasis is on the use of community resources to meet community objectives. Some studies shed light on success that can be expected from this approach. In the 1950s Back and Hurt [2] researched the organization of resources among low-income farms in eastern Oklahoma and concluded that even the most efficient combination of resources using optimal management and technology could not bring the acceptable level of income to operators of these farms within their current fence boundaries. Schultz [17] argues that traditional societies are already sufficiently close to an optimal use of resources that a more nearly efficient combination of resources would not raise incomes perceptibly. Outside assistance in the form of capital and new technology is essential. Conclusions similar to those reached by Back, Hurt, and Schultz likely hold for many depressed communities and areas in the United States. Communities cannot pull themselves up by their rotted bootstraps and must look outward as well as inward. Looking inward means organizing the community to get the most out of local initiative and resources. Looking outward means using outside technology and capital.

A second problem is that defining development as a *process* confuses the medium with the message, the means with the end. Emphasis on improving community organization to meet community objectives has led to misguided and weak programs. This is apparent as we look at the genesis of national programs for micropolitan development. In the 1930s the Resettlement Administration and Farm Security Administration tried to improve rural communities. Interest in development revived in the 1950s with the Rural Development Program (RDP) which emphasized self-help toward meeting objectives uniquely specified by each community. It was argued that the community is best able to identify its problems and to work out the solutions using community leadership, community resources, and existing programs largely designed for commercial farmers. Emphasis was on forming rural development committees composed of local community leaders. The program was not successful in bringing micropolitan development.

A similar approach was used by the Kennedy and Johnson administrations in the Rural Area Development program. This program, like RDP, was largely a pilot effort that produced few tangible, lasting results. Lessons should have been learned from these two failures, but the Nixon administration once again established rural development committees to promote development through self-help. Communities and their leaders too often were abandoned once committees were organized.[1] None of these efforts at development on the part of the USDA and land-grant institutions brought people to jobs or jobs to people. The efforts brought some community improvement and improved services but not much development in the form of higher incomes. Cynics might contend that the programs were an economical attempt to create the illusion of action with no real commitment to micropolitan development. These past efforts to make micropolis into "bedroom" communities that are good places to live but not to work only create communities that are good for neither.

The proposed cabinet reorganization to bring all community development activities under one new department is laudatory. But of special concern for the land-grant institution researchers who have not worked closely with the U.S. Departments of Commerce, Labor, and HEW is that this reorganization may strip from the USDA the last vestiges of programs (FHA, REA, SCS, food stamps, and rural development research) to serve the entire micropolitan community. Will commercial farmers have sufficient political power to sustain a USDA stripped of its broader programs? What will be the new roles of the Cooperative State Research Service, agricultural experiment stations, and the cooperative extension service?

1. Failure to enact an adequate micropolitan development policy arises to a large degree from lack of a vocal and organized constituency to support such policies. The extension service gave birth to the American Farm Bureau Federation through early organization of commercial farmers. So too, the most enduring contribution of the extension service in micropolitan development could be to spawn an "American Micropolitan Bureau Federation" out of the development committees that have been organized.

The cooperative extension service can point to some success in organizing rural leadership. Lack of research shares blame for failure to follow up community organization with action. Researchers have not adequately perceived the "global" aspects of micropolitan development. The process was viewed as a labor-intensive activity: sending enough personnel to help the local community would bring development. In fact micropolitan development is a capital-intensive activity. Community development efforts have gotten ahead of the national policies, research, planning, and capital required to make them work; more policy research must be devoted to devising optimal state and national policies that provide capital and planning to follow through local efforts. If the research fails to spur state and national commitment of capital, at least it may lead to better organization of existing program resources.

Research on local issues also needs to be changed, in some cases toward research teams or task forces to follow up on community organization. This requires short-term planning and unsophisticated "brushfire" research. Much of the effort in community resource development attempts to provide better medical, educational, recreational, and housing facilities. While such efforts improve the community, the perspective of those concerned with development must be broadened to place greater emphasis on improving *incomes* and *job opportunities* for micropolitan people.[2]

Bringing People to Jobs. Bringing people to jobs has been by far the largest, albeit de facto, program to raise incomes of micropolitan people. Some economists, observing that outmigration has reduced per capita income of the sending and receiving area, have concluded that outmigration should not be encouraged. Defining micropolitan development as an increase in income or well-being of micropolitan people wherever they eventually reside, outmigration has been a resounding success. If the income of people who left micropolis is averaged with the income of people who remain, outmigration has markedly raised income of micropolitan people. It perhaps has reduced average income in the receiving area but has increased national per capita income, hence it is a policy to pursue vigorously. Measured by income, housing, community services, schooling for children, and other measures, migrants fare much better in the city than in the

2. Income is not all-important, but it is the means to many important health, food, housing, and other factors influencing the quality of life. Perhaps instead of saying we know what is best for people by providing one program for housing, another for food, and another for medical services, we should concentrate on raising incomes and let people make their own choices concerning the level and combination of goods and services they wish to consume. Much bureaucracy and many unmanageable programs would be eliminated.

rural community which they left [21]. Of course proper programs could have better prepared them for the great rural-urban exodus. We must avoid being trapped in programs to save communities rather than people.

Expansion of federal-state employment service activities seems warranted. Research is needed to determine what level of activity is economically feasible: additional job counseling, training, subsidized mobility, etc. A recent study [12] evaluated the economic payoff from the subsidized mobility demonstration projects carried out in a number of states in the 1960s. Some of these pilot projects had a negative rate of return on public investment, but the rate of return over all projects averaged nearly 30 percent. While more extensive labor mobility subsidies have been used in Canada and Western European countries with success, one disturbing finding from the American experience was the high rate of backmigration to the sending area. Sometimes it comprised two-thirds of the relocatees and averaged approximately 30 percent backmigration annually. Improved counseling, selection, training, and other services along with grouping together the people from a sending area in the receiving area reduces backmigration rates. Still the results clearly show that many people induced to migrate elsewhere have an undeterable homing instinct; others cannot be moved at all. Thus policies to bring people to jobs must attend programs to bring jobs to people.

Bringing Jobs to People. One study [21] concluded that the nation has followed a powerful de facto policy of centralization. Federal outlays per capita have been high at the extreme ends of the population density spectrum—in open country and in large metropolitan cities. The payments in the open country were largely for commercial farmers. Commodity programs provided capital and security to large farmers which enhanced their competitive position and pushed the small farmer, hired worker, and sharecropper from the farm. Declining farming opportunities also meant declining nonfarm rural job opportunities. On the other hand, large government payments to metropolitan areas were for government facilities, payrolls, and welfare. These policies created jobs and favorable economic incentives, pulling people to the metropolis. The combined push-pull efforts constituted a major policy of centralization.

Many of us hold the value judgment that policies promoting decentralization are desirable, but we have had little objective research to back this judgment. A recent study [11] examines economies of city size, estimating the cost per capita of providing community services including pollution control; crime and fire protection; and water, sewage, garbage, and electricity. Results indicate that the per capita cost of providing a given quality of community services is lowest in cities of 50,000–750,000 population. This study alone cannot be taken as a final answer to the question of what size of city should be encouraged in decentralization policies. Other data on private cost of production and social attitudes by city size will provide a more complete basis for establishing policies. Though it seems unlikely, anomie and racial injustice may be more severe problems in the economically optimal size cities.

A study [18] of industries that have located in the Ozark region of eastern Oklahoma since 1960 indicated that the community could afford to subsidize industry by $3,800 annually per new job created and just break even. That is, the community could pay that amount to industry and be just as well off as without new jobs. The study was unique, looking not only at the benefits in the form of payroll and secondary effects but also at the costs measured by additional utilities and school services required for new residents. The study also considered the people who would have gone elsewhere for jobs if the industry had not located. Results showed that not all sectors gained. In several instances the school and municipal government sectors experienced a net loss despite large gains to the private sector. Additional taxes attributed to new firms were insufficient to cover the cost of schooling added students and of concessions granted the firms. Some individuals were made worse off because higher tax rates to pay added school and utility costs were borne in part by people who did not benefit from new jobs.

While studies indicate that the benefits are large from bringing jobs to people, some economists [8, 9] contend that "hothouse" efforts in the form of tax and other concessions to attract industry have failed. On the other hand, experience in Puerto Rico with "Operation Bootstrap" indicates tax incentives can draw industry and jobs.

Not all micropolitan communities are suited for industry. The concept of a micropolitan development district is important; a small community that faces declining employment opportunities is less alienated if it sees itself as part of an overall effort to attract industry to a center of sufficient size to provide economies of operation to firms, community services at low cost, jobs within reach of hinterland micropolitan workers, and a growing population.

Despite favorable arguments for decentralization and bringing jobs within commuting distance of micropolitan people, public policy has not responded except with weak programs of low-interest loans and with grants to improve community services. Powerful interest groups oppose strong programs to bring jobs to micropolitan people. These interest groups include labor unions and industry in metropolis who see decentralization of industry as "robbing Peter to pay Paul." Telling opposition comes also from micropolitan areas, where established industries see subsidies to new industry as a threat.

To foster a more progressive distribution of benefits from public programs, the federal government must assume much of the burden for subsidizing industry location. Lack of resources places micropolitan growth centers, which most need and benefit from new jobs, in a poor position to provide incentives. A program of tax write-offs or other means to attract industry may need to be accompanied by incentives for locating firms to hire the most disadvantaged. Many micropolitan people have already failed at jobs in the metropolis; the same characteristics mitigate against success in high-paying new jobs in micropolitan communities. Evidence indicates that the criteria being used by the Economic Department Administration and other agencies to promote development discriminate against rural people [21].

Finally, research is needed to determine what industries and government facilities are suitable for location in micropolitan communities. Estimates are needed of the supply curve of new jobs created for alternative levels of subsidy provided to complement the demand analysis indicating how far a community can afford to go in providing incentives to new industries.

Transfer Payments. One form of transfer payments to micropolitan communities is compensation for net spillout of capital in the form of investment in education of outmigrants. Studies [8, 9] indicate that a large portion of investment in education made by economically depressed areas leaves the area. Net spillout of schooling constitutes a large transfer of capital from micropolis to metropolis.

While neither economists nor micropolitan people tend to view public assistance as a development program, the Family Assistance Plan perhaps would do more for the well-being of residents of micropolitan areas than any other single national policy. Furthermore, it would retard the flow of micropolitan residents to urban ghettos. Few land-grant institutions are researching such issues.

NORMATIVE RESEARCH FRAMEWORK. Allocating research resources with a highly refined normative model is a worthy but distant and elusive goal. The sophisticated analysis of research resources can best be reached in phases as described below.

Phase I: Problem Inventory. Most research in micropolitan development has inventoried existing conditions; this phase began as early as the 1790 census. Phase I is continuing, with impressive contributions not only by the Bureau of Census but also by the Economic Development Division of the Economic Research Service in the USDA, which is also performing very well indeed in other phases of research.

Many land-grant universities have continued this tradition with numerous personal interview surveys of rural areas and communities. While the need to identify problems and their dimensions continues, economists must progress beyond the inventory phase to arrive at solutions to micropolitan problems.

Phase II: Planning Programs. Origins of the second phase of micropolitan development research—planning programs—can be traced to the 1930s with numerous New Deal programs. This effort was dampened by World War II, then revived in the USDA with the Farmers Home Administration and later with the Rural Development Program. Planning of programs proliferated beyond reason during the Kennedy and Johnson administrations. The Area Redevelopment Administration originating in the Kennedy administration gave way to the Economic Development Administration and Manpower Development and Training Administration. These programs, along with those of the Office of Economic Opportunity and the Department of Health, Education and Welfare, demonstrated growing public commitment to micropolitan development. More importantly, they signaled a new direction in programs: major programs for micropolitan development would be administered not by the USDA but by other departments and agencies for rural and urban sectors alike. These new programs lacked coordination and resulted in a balkanization that precluded efficient use of funds and a critical mass of resources to deal with any one problem. From 1960 to 1968 the number of domestic federal programs increased from 45 to 435 [4, p. 4]. The 1970 Executive Office Catalog of Federal Domestic Assistance listed over 1,000 separate programs. Programs intended for rural and urban areas tended to slight the former [21].

While effort to coordinate programs at the local level has been uplifted by the Office of Management and Budget Circular A-95 (which gives Economic Development Districts and individual states leverage in coordinating federal funds), programs remain fragmented and nonadditive. They accomplish ends not envisioned and foster demographic centralization [21]. The time has come to turn from discordant programs to an orchestrated development policy—to interrupt planning programs and start programming plans.

Phase III: Programming Plans. Economic development district planners as well as state and national policy makers seek an overall framework for micropolitan development research to improve data gathering and to make research more relevant in planning action programs. They are essentially asking, "What level and combination of public program can reach prescribed development targets at least public expense?" Economists yet lack the answer, but the following normative framework is designed to provide the structure for guiding needed research. A more nearly comprehensive structure for allocating research resources rather than public programs is presented later as Phase IV.

The following model for programming plans has been outlined elsewhere [19], and some of the coefficients needed to make it operational are available [16, Ch. 14]. The objective of micropolitan development can be conceptualized as maximizing net income of a population or area with limited public funds available for programs to promote development. Or the objective might be to minimize the public cost of reaching certain development targets such as desired levels of employment, income, and stability. One goal in a planning model might be to reach at least a poverty threshold income for the poor. The model should contain a wide range of available public programs including subsidized migration, technical and general education, industry location incentives, payments to private industry to train and employ the disadvantaged, investment in social overhead, family planning, and various public assistance programs with some providing work incentives. Emphasis is on the level and combination of these programs to reach development targets efficiently rather than showing (as do many current simulation planning models) what happens to aggregate income when a sector is expanded without regard to rates of return and how public policies can stimulate each sector. The focus is on efficient use of public funds, but private investment is frequently complementary. In fact public funds are likely to be most effective in raising incomes where they induce considerable private investment.

One of the possible models for devising a development strategy in the above context is linear programming. The objective function (1) expresses the total public cost Z as a function of the specific program level x_j times the public cost per unit of that program c_j. In matrix notation:

$$\text{Min} \quad Z = CX' \tag{1}$$

where C and X are row vectors of c_j and x_j respectively. Constraints in the model are designated by a column vector B. The row constraints include the number of the population in various demographic and work-eligibility categories and the income and other targets for a specific category. The "technical" coefficients a_{ij} indicate the impact of public policy j on the subsystem population in row i. The public cost Z is minimized subject to constraints that income and other targets be equal to or greater than prescribed levels as in (2) where A is the matrix of technical coefficients.

$$AX' \geqq B \tag{2}$$

The final constraint is that the public policy activities be at nonnegative levels:

$$x_j \geqq 0 \tag{3}$$

Dynamic, polyperiod, or nonlinear programming might improve the model. Simulation techniques could provide even more flexibility and allow analysis of the system over an extended period of time. Simulation with population cohorts could reflect the impact in subsequent generations of, for example, family planning policies in the current generation. Experimentation with various models could reveal which formulation is best suited to devise a development strategy.

The geographic unit chosen for economic development planning ordinarily will encompass at least a multicounty economic development district or a multidistrict region such as the Ozarks. The county, township, or town unit is too small for devising strategy if national public policy changes are an issue.

The model finds the optimal combination of programs that uses limited public funds efficiently while meeting targets geared to unique characteristics of a heterogeneous population. Emphasis in early years might be on public assistance type of programs until programs such as family planning, job creation, induced migration, and education ranking higher in long-term cost effectiveness have had time to realize their impact.

Industrial location incentives, long-term land retirement, and general education may efficiently raise micropolitan income but are frequently regressive in character; they disproportionately concentrate benefits on those who least need special public help. This problem can be handled in the design of a programming model having an objective function that maximizes income of an area. The population is merely divided into various categories with restraints that income attain at least some minimum level for the most disadvantaged. The shadow prices indicate the loss in aggregate income in the entire area stemming from such constraints. The results quantitatively illustrate the tradeoff between efficiency (maximum aggregate income from program budget) and equity (favorable distribution of income).

The above model has a hearty appetite for data. Characteristics of the population in the planning area must be detailed. Data must show how alternative programs operated at various levels influence each of many subpopulations. This requires information on the distribution of program benefits and a schedule of efficiency—a considerable departure from existing statistics which provide a point estimate of efficiency (benefit-cost ratio, rate of return, or cost effectiveness coefficient) and seldom any information on the distribution of benefits among subpopulations.

Phase IV: Programming Allocation of Research Resources. Development of a rigorous analytical framework to allocate research resources to micropolitan development is much more difficult conceptually and operationally than devising the framework to allocate public programs. Estimating the direct payoff from action programs is a challenge; estimating the payoff from research to improve action programs is a greater challenge. Some conceptual problems have been outlined [20].

Characteristics of agricultural experiment station research that portend problems in adjusting resources are cited by Robinson [15]:

1. Only a small proportion of resources allocated to research has a direct economic effect on small-scale or part-time farmers, rural persons leaving farming, or rural residents not employed in the agricultural industry, despite the fact that rural nonfarmers make up three-fourths of the total rural population.
2. Experiment station research is predominantly directed to problems in primary agricultural production, not to problems beyond the farm gate.
3. The research is heavily committed to the biological sciences. In 1965 the stations allocated 78 percent of all funds to biological research, 14 percent to physical sciences research, and 8 percent to social science research.
4. Experiment station research allocation exhibits surprising stability among areas over time. Although the number of personnel increased 200 percent from 1930 to 1967, the proportion of personnel devoted to each area of research changed almost imperceptibly over the period.

As reasons for the stability in research expenditure shares, Robinson cites the planning process of experiment stations wherein the distribution of funds among departments and disciplines tends to be taken as given. Redirection of resources largely occurs within departments or disciplines. Stability of research shares is also explained by the composition of advisory groups which are established along commodity and industry lines. These groups are oriented toward traditional research needs. The rural nonfarmer, the small farmer, the leaders of rural communities, and the consumer are not usually represented on the experiment station advisory committees.

The programming, planning, and budgeting (PPB) approach allows for various levels of sophistication in research planning. One level is the use of program budgets as opposed to project or agency budgets. A second level is use of cost effectiveness, cost-benefit, or rate-of-return measurements to allocate research to areas offering best results. A third level may be viewed as systems planning, which entails the above two levels but also emphasizes a wholistic view of the problem areas, alternative strategies for accomplishing research objectives, and an integrated overall program to use the optimal amount and mix of research resources that deal efficiently with the problem area.

The PPB approach has been used widely within the federal government to improve decisions. Use of program budgets rather than agency or project budgets appears to be of some value to decision makers. Williamson [22] reports on the joint USDA and state experiment station study [1] of research needs using a program budget of scientific man-years. Although an early effort was made to define the goals of research, this effort was not very successful; final agreement on goals was not reached until the estimation of future research needs was essentially complete. Each of 91 problem areas was rated by the panels on a scale of 1 to 5 according to how well each category met eight criteria of desirability. These scores then were multiplied by the respective weights for each category. But Williamson says,

> I do not believe the use of this scoring device had any appreciable effect on the final estimates of research needs in 1972 and 1977 [22, p. 297]. . . . The practicing scientist commonly views with suspicion any suggestion that his work is amenable to a cost-benefit estimation procedure. To most, and this also includes economists, the very suggestion smacks of vulgar commercialism on something sacred [22, p. 300].

The panels recommended that micropolitan development research be increased relative to the production-oriented research for commercial farmers. But the proposed increase in scientific man-years between 1965 and 1977 was 3,230 for efficient production of farm and forest products and protection of forest, crops, and livestock compared to only 1,272 for raising levels of living of rural people and improving community services and environment [1, p. 188].

The program budget is an appropriate beginning; the PPB framework expanded to cost-benefit or cost effectiveness analysis requires more sophisticated examination of costs and/or benefits from research than does a program budget. Schultz [16, p. 91] emphasizes that research requires scarce resources and produces something of value, therefore it is an economic activity. The scarce resources are readily observable and not difficult to measure, but the link between input and output and the appropriate value to place on the output are elusive quantities indeed.

Paulsen [13, pp. 80, 81] states: "To place a rough, relative and even absolute value on different research must be possible because it is done all the time (by administrators, politicians, and researchers). . . . The question is not whether but how well and by whom research output should be appraised."

Bayley [3, p. 231] calls for better measures of who benefits and who loses from research as a first requirement for useful cost-benefit analysis. He notes considerable progress in developing a program-oriented structure for research but little progress in applying systems analysis techniques of cost effectiveness or cost-benefit in evaluation of technological alternatives for solution of specific research problems; he holds little hope for such applications in evaluating specific research projects.

Puterbaugh [14] describes the application of PPB in Agricultural Research Service (ARS) planning where PPB has concentrated on the relative value of alternative technological objectives using cost-benefit analysis. No attempt has been made to apply a cost effectiveness analysis to research—that is, to determine the type and quantity best suited for attaining some given technological objective. No attempt at cost effectiveness analysis is planned in this area; the subjective estimates by scientists are believed to be the most accurate [14, pp. 324–25]. Approximately 10 percent of research programs received an economic analysis that is usable in decision making. Little progress has been made in shifting the emphasis away from analysis of incremental proposals to look at the entire program; a zero-base budget is still not an operational reality in ARS. Also, little work has been done on constructing a long-term, multiyear research budget in ARS, according to Puterbaugh.

Mahlstede [10] reports on long-range planning at the Iowa Agricultural and Home Economics Experiment Station. The evaluation was within the framework of a single goal—growth. A five-year plan for three different budget levels was the product of the study using a detailed cost estimation procedure but no quantified estimates of benefits. The problem of equity, though important, was set aside for the initial analysis because of the difficulty in measuring and weighting this goal in relation to the goal of growth.

While we continue to refine program budgeting and cost effectiveness analysis of individual programs, it is useful to conceptualize an ideal systems framework which considers a more global accounting of research strategies, joint objectives of efficiency and equity, and interactions. The need to consider objectives other than efficiency is emphasized by Heady [9, p. 135]:

> At what point should the stream of research resources directed at increased productivity and diminished resource inputs be diverted toward solving the important social problems generated by them? . . . There is a great need for a broad delineation of equity problems by agricultural

scientists and administrators, as well as for the continued development of models of resource allocations, to provide equitable distributions of the gains from farm technological advance.

A conceptual normative systems framework for allocating research resources to promote micropolitan development can be viewed initially at least as a linear programming problem:

$$\text{Max} \quad Z = CX' \tag{4}$$
$$AX' > B \tag{5}$$
$$x_j > 0 \tag{6}$$

The objective function (4) is essentially a social welfare function, where X is a row vector of subpopulations in the micropolitan population and intermediate activities delineated for planning purposes. Each x_j $(j = m + 1 \text{ to } k)$ represents a relatively homogeneous subpopulation similar in age, education, and other socioeconomic-demographic characteristics. Ordinarily research is not an action program but helps to guide action programs. Hence intermediate activities are called for, with research activities x_j $(j = 1 \text{ to } n)$ contributing to action programs x_j $(j = n + 1 \text{ to } m)$ which in turn contribute to income or well-being of subpopulation x_j $(j = m + 1 \text{ to } k)$.

The c_j for each subpopulation is dollar increments in income and for the intermediate activities is cost of each unit of the activity. To make (4) more nearly the social welfare function that it ideally should be, the c_j can be measured in dollars adjusted for the marginal utility of money using normative judgments based (for example) on federal income tax rates, the proportion of income spent for necessities in each economic class, or a logarithmic transformation of income. These adjustments seem crude but should be no less acceptable than the current fashion of assuming that marginal utility of money is constant and the same for all individuals and levels of income.

Institutional constraints including the views of administrators, legislators, and the public frequently circumscribe the kinds of research that can be undertaken to promote micropolitan development. The column vector B of restraints indicates availability of research personnel, funds, and institutions. Research personnel and funds must be taken as given in the short run, but intermediate activities can be inserted into the model that allocate funds to train more research personnel who in turn contribute to the objective function.

The technical coefficients a_{ij} in the A matrix indicate the contribution of research and other inputs to activity x_j. The production function for a given action program can be divided into several activities representing various levels of research to accommodate diminishing returns.

In allocating research, costs or inputs are the easiest to identify. Enormous problems arise in determining the value of output, which might be viewed as the value of benefits from research multiplied by the probability of success associated with alternative input levels. Pitfalls in estimating benefits are large in physical sciences and even larger in social sciences.

The usual refinements in static linear programming appear warranted. Time required to show the impact of additional research resources and training of more scientists, as well as long-term impacts of programs such as family planning on future generations, calls for dynamic or polyperiod analysis. Diminishing returns on marginal utilities call for nonlinear programming. Lumpiness of some resources (such as research personnel) suggest advantages in integer programming, and uncertainties that characterize many coefficients in the model call for stochastic programming. Parametric programming, varying the funding restraint, would help trace out a marginal value product (MVP) curve for research and permit determination of an optimal research outlay—the point at which the MVP equals the opportunity cost of money.

Complexities of using a sophisticated normative model to allocate research resources are obvious. While no attempt has been made or is likely to be made for some time to apply the above systems model, a model of research planning containing some of the refinements of the ideal model was formulated and applied by Fishel [7] and is labeled the Minnesota Agricultural Research Resource Allocation Information System (MARRAIS). After experimenting with MARRAIS in actual use, he concludes: "We are a long way from seeing such techniques being employed as *the* allocator of research resources. Neither the current state of development of allocative techniques nor the temperament of the research establishment in the public sector is up to what would be required of them" [7, p. 379].

REFERENCES

1. Association of State Universities and Land Grant Colleges and U.S. Department of Agriculture, *A National Program of Research for Agriculture,* USDA, Oct. 1966.
2. Back, W. B., and Verner Hurt, *Potential for Agricultural Adjustment in the Ouachita Highlands of Oklahoma,* Okla. Agr. Exp. Sta. Bull. B-582, 1961.
3. Bayley, Ned, "Research resource allocation in the Department of Agriculture," in Fishel, Walter (ed.), *Resource Allocation in Agricultural Research* (Minneapolis: Univ. Minn. Press, 1971), pp. 218–34.
4. Daft, Lynn, *Framework for Rural Development Policies and Programs: Is This the Real Thing?* Proc. Southern Agr. Econ. Assn., 1972.
5. Extension Committee on Organization and Policy, *Community Resource Development,* Cooperative Extension Service, USDA, 1967.

6. Fishel, Walter (ed.), *Resource Allocation in Agricultural Research* (Minneapolis: Univ. Minn. Press, 1971).
7. Fishel, Walter, "The Minnesota agricultural research resource allocation information system and experiment," in Fishel (ed.), pp. 344–81.
8. Hansen, Niles, "Regional development and the rural poor," *J. Human Resources*, 4:205–14, 1969.
9. Heady, Earl, "Welfare implications for agricultural research," in Fishel (ed.), pp. 121–36.
10. Mahlstede, John, "Long-range planning at the Iowa Agricultural and Home Economics Experiment Station," in Fishel (ed.), pp. 326–43.
11. Morris, Douglas, *Economies of City Size: Per Capita Costs of Providing Community Services,* unpublished Ph.D. thesis, Okla. State Univ., 1972.
12. Nelson, James, *Subsidized Labor Mobility—An Alternative Use of Development Funds* (mimeo), Dept. Agr. Econ., Okla. State Univ., 1972.
13. Paulsen, Arnold, "The pricing of research output," in Fishel (ed.), pp. 80–89.
14. Puterbaugh, Horace, "An application of PPB in the Agricultural Research Service," in Fishel (ed.), pp. 316–25.
15. Robinson, Roland, "Resource allocation in the land-grant universities and agricultural experiment station," in Fishel (ed.), pp. 235–50.
16. Schultz, T. W., "The allocation of resources to research," in Fishel (ed.), pp. 90–120.
17. Schultz, T. W., *Transforming Traditional Agriculture* (New Haven, Conn.: Yale Univ. Press, 1964).
18. Shaffer, Ronald. *The Net Economic Impact of New Industry on Rural Communities in Eastern Oklahoma,* unpublished Ph.D. thesis, Okla. State Univ., 1972.
19. Tweeten, Luther, "Applying welfare economic theory to rural development research," in Garnett Bradford and Fred Saunders (eds.), *Quantitative Techniques with Application to Rural Development Research,* Southern Farm Management Research Committee and Farm Foundation, pp. 21–42, 1972.
20. Tweeten, Luther, "The search for a theory and methodology of research resource allocation," in Fishel (ed.), pp. 25–61.
21. Tweeten, Luther, and Daryll Ray, *Impact of Public Compensation Policies* (mimeo), Dept. Agr. Econ., Okla. State Univ., 1972.
22. Williamson, J. C., Jr., "The joint Department of Agriculture and state experiment station study of research needs," in Fishel (ed.), pp. 289–301.

CHAPTEN TEN

ORGANIZATION OF UNIVERSITY PERSONNEL

R. L. KOHLS

HOW CAN WE stimulate effective research activity that will improve the development and progress of our rural communities? As we break down this broad and important question, two aspects of the problem emerge: (1) How can we more effectively encourage researchers to attack relevant and important problems that occur as we pursue the general area of development and progress of our rural communities? (2) What are these problems, and what is their nature and dimension?

The first of these is a people and people-management question, centering around how we might organize to get the job done. The second is a content question, and answers will have to be evolved by competent people as they become interested in the problem.

Our biggest assets in agricultural education are the institutions of the experiment station and the cooperative extension service as separate, viable organizational frameworks. The Hatch Act did not simply fund research as one of the missions of the land-grant university; it established in each college "a department to be known and designated as an Agricultural Experiment Station," and the duty of such stations was "to conduct researches and verify experiments to solve problems of agricultural production and related issues." The Smith-Lever Act did not simply fund adult education as one of the missions of the university; it brought into being a separate organization that was to act as the teaching and delivery system of research findings to those who were not on the college campuses but who were practitioners and users of the information that might develop on these campuses. In both instances there were only vague references to the

R. L. KOHLS is Dean of Agriculture, Purdue University, Lafayette, Ind.

teaching functions normally assigned to the university. In both instances every legislature placed these two major organizational devices—the experiment station and the cooperative extension service—at the land-grant university under its jurisdiction but on a semiautonomous status. They were to be subject to federal coordination and direction but operate under their own independent administrators, who were to be approved jointly by the university representing the state and by the federal government. This is probably the first and certainly most successful example of the revenue sharing and fund matching concept of different levels of government we have. It has resulted in the effective joining of local direction and local problem identification, with the responsibility assigned at a national level to help give coordination, direction, and purpose.

In our early history these two organizations were characterized by a sharp delineation of their staffs: the school had its staff for teaching, the experiment station had its staff for research, and the extension service had its staff to carry out its adult education duties. At Purdue the station and extension staffs were not formally joined completely to the university staffs until after World War II. Many universities had buildings especially designed for their experiment stations and their laboratory. Early in this development, research personnel often reported to the same head as the school personnel. Extension directors relinquished direct control of their staffs much more recently, and some have not done this yet.

The present blurring of the functions of a university faculty as "teaching, research, and extension," the joint appointments of faculty into these missions, and the highly powerful and semiautonomous units called departments are developments of rather recent vintage in the agricultural college setup. Although they are joined at department levels, the experiment station director is still responsible for the performance of the research structure, and the extension director is still responsible for the performance of the extension education program. Both the federal and state governments use these institutional vehicles often to direct the efforts of the research establishment and the adult education establishment into what Congress and individual state legislatures view as important problems of the public interest. This has come about with funds earmarked for specific purposes, and various legislatures have made appropriations to get certain activities done.

ROLE OF THE DEPARTMENT. It is often stated that the keys to a truly great university are: (1) a faculty of competent, vigorous individuals and (2) strong and competent department heads to administer this basic organization. One often hears that the best run university is the one that assembles the most capable people and simply lets them devote their talents to things that interest them.

A major legitimatizing mechanism to evaluate faculty performance has developed that is external to the institution. This consists of the many organizations that surround the disciplines and professions. Each discipline and profession has its own national society. Many areas have developed accrediting agencies that determine whether or not an institution is pursuing the correct path. For many of the faculty the most important recognition may come from outside their university.

Many of these developments that surround the academic freedom of the individual and the power and autonomy of the departmental and disciplinary organizations are at least partially responsible for our national educational success and progress. They are also responsible for at least some of the roadblocks and difficulties that face universities and academia in general as they adapt and change to new dimensions. Some of the results have not been good, and some of the statements and assumptions made previously are not completely true.

Several recent developments indicate that the present structure is not without its problems. The complaints of students in the last several years in many ways were protests against out-of-date and duplicatory courses and general academic neglect of the teaching function. Students and others have charged that faculty people, running their own show, have become far too interested in pursuing their own interests and their own research devices with little attention to the primary mission of the university—teaching students. The public is demanding more direction, responsibility, and accountability in the general operations of academia. One notes the growth of coordinating superboards in various states and the many national commissions that are identifying problems and legislative proposals to correct these alleged shortcomings.

The idea of "doing what you please" on the part of the faculty has often been followed by "if you can find the money." Fundamentally the faculty could do as they pleased, provided some granting agency agreed with them as to the area they desired to pursue. Whether we like it or not, most granting agencies—federal, private foundations, or private businesses—have used their funds for a purpose. History demonstrates that in this atmosphere most faculty are quite adept at coordinating their pleasures with the money sources.

However, this laissez-faire philosophy has never been completely dominant in the agricultural organization of the land-grant university. Both the experiment station and the extension service have vocal clientele who clamor to have some input into the nature of the programs that are to service them. Most states have found that it is unwise for a unit to completely ignore these voices of supporters, users, and interested clientele for very long.

Additional money at both state and federal levels has often been appropriated into the research and extension structures with both purpose and earmarking of funds. Only recently the Agricultural Marketing Act designated its funds for specific purposes. In the early stages the experiment station directors and others jumped through all sorts of definitional hoops so that they might use these monies just to support the programs going on at the time. The real challenge was to define the marketing purpose in such a way that things that experiment stations were doing fell in this category! However, in spite of this, change eventually did occur in most universities to give more research emphasis to marketing problems.

In large segments of the university, departments are synonymous with disciplines such as English, history, chemistry, and physics. These departments can easily wrap the protective cloak of disciplinary power around them in their behavior. However, this discipline-department arrangement in agriculture is at best a tenuous one. One has merely to survey the organizational charts of agricultural colleges around the country to recognize how diverse they are in this regard. For example, at Purdue we have one department of animal sciences. However, another major school has departments of animal science, dairy science, food and dairy industry, genetics, and poultry science. At Purdue we have departments of horticulture, agronomy, and botany and plant pathology. These basic disciplinary and mission areas at some other universities may be organized into departments of pomology, vegetable crops, floriculture and ornamental horticulture, crop science, botany, genetics, and soil science.

We must not get caught in the trap of letting policies of protecting and supporting disciplines be twisted into a rationale for supporting the organizational status quo. Purdue has chosen the organizational route of a few but large departmental units. There are nine of these departmental units, of which at least seven house a collection of disciplinary orientations and allegiance. Other universities have chosen the route of having many departments more narrowly defined. The important point is that the department is an organizational unit for getting a job done. The discipline defines a conceptual area of attention. A department may contain several disciplinary groups dedicated to a single mission or problem area.

How should we organize to give increased attention to community and rural development? The question is not *whether* the school, experiment station, and extension service will accept the challenge of this mission but rather *how* the challenge will be accepted.

What is community and rural development? Is it a new discipline that has simply not been fully developed? Or is it a special mission area in which many disciplines will have to be involved? Bryce Ratchford, who has considered this matter rather extensively from many viewpoints, has said that development is about as broad as the total concerns of man. But he also stated that community development is a new profession. Some institutions have established new departments to administer this thrust. A professional Society of Community Development has been born; it has its own journal and is developing its own disciplinary paraphernalia. Contributions to this new journal include offerings from educational psychologists, sociologists, anthropologists, agricultural economists, consumer economists, lawyers, businessmen, and political scientists.

What is the content of this problem area? What are its research problems? At the present time we are not sure, but this should not limit effective action. When economics broke off from political economy or when agricultural economics broke off from economics itself, the people who were involved in these initial ventures did not know precisely the dimension of the field they were claiming as a new discipline. The birth of many of our "agricultural disciplines" was not from a specific dimension of an academic area but from a concern over a problem and a mission that was not being well handled under old disciplinary structures.

The most important action is for deans, directors of experiment stations and extension services, and other faculty leaders to make the visible decision that rural community development is an area of high concern and importance to rural people and that evolving national policy will make it a valid mission for teaching, research, and extension attention. Once this commitment is made, we must be prepared to take academic actions that involve risk. We must be prepared to make allocation decisions as the opportunities arise to bring resources to bear on this mission. We cannot logically take the position that we will move only if given more money to do this specific job. Obviously this is the easiest route, and we all hope additional resources will be available. However, if we do receive money to strengthen our commitment to this area, we cannot again play the old game of redefining development so we can support in a better fashion just what we are doing now. It is an unescapable conclusion that to undertake this as a mission of high priority means that in most of our institutions, some redirection and reallocation of personnel and resources are necessary.

RESTRUCTURING ACADEMIA. What organizational approaches are in order? This is a pragmatic question that must be answered in the framework of the history and structure of each institution. If the historic structure of the institution is one of many small and changing departments, each with a rather specific and narrow mission, then perhaps a new departmental organization is in order. If the structure is one of large multimission and multidisciplinary units, adjustments may be needed within that framework. If the history of the institution is one that widely utilizes institutes and other nondepartmental devices for handling specific problems, this may be the route. Any move that is made, however, must combine the authority and responsibility of the teaching, research, and extension functions. Separate research institutes that do not include consideration of the other two missions are inadequate; curricula and educational efforts must also be developed. We will also need field agents in our extension services, and these people will need special training. It is important that extension and research personnel be kept together at this stage of uncertainty; communication and interplay must be close. Perhaps in more instances than not, these functions should be combined within the same person. In most states community development extension activities and concern are further along than research.

In research it is extremely important that we undertake a program of carefully chosen efforts. Too often researchers simply become the fire brigade to put out the fires that extension brings to them. If all our research talents are utilized on ad hoc problems, we cannot begin to develop a systematic body of knowledge that is of predictive and future importance. Researchers must acknowledge the major problems that extension faces and take them into consideration when planning their efforts.

PURDUE'S FORMULA. As an example and not as a model, I will outline what we are attempting at Purdue. It should be remembered that Purdue has a philosophy of few and large multidisciplinary departments. The office of Program Director of Rural Community Development has been established and put in charge of the development of teaching, research, and extension functions that surround this problem area as they pertain to agriculture. Faculty have volunteered to the program if their interests are involved. They are appointed specifically to the Rural Community Development Program faculty but retain their basic appointments in their home departments. The faculty currently includes local government and community-oriented people from agricultural economics, landscape architecture, and urban planning; land use and land engineering people from agronomy and agricultural engineering; recreation and natural resource people from forestry; and youth people from 4-H.

The program director and this faculty are empowered to act like a department in matters of curricula, research, and extension program planning and in relationships with the field staff. I depend upon this faculty and the program director to determine the general specifications for needed new personnel and to identify into which department and discipline they best belong. We have recently added two sociologists and a social psychologist to the Department of Agricultural Economics. This faculty has its own seminars, has its own committee structure, seeks grants supportive to the programs, and has its own small budget for travel and speakers.

Basically it is intended that the personnel and research support will flow back through the best related department structure. I do have the authority, however, to appoint people directly into the program faculty if the cooperation breaks down in needed areas. This program structure is one of three we have in agriculture. Food science and environmental science and natural resources are two other such cross-departmental program faculties that we have.

Will it work? Must it evolve into a department sometime in the future? Only time will tell. The departments themselves are giving cooperation in various degrees. In order to enhance the ability of these program faculties to deal with their problems, I insist upon input from program faculties and the director in the allocation of resources, promotion of personnel, and other ongoing administrative devices.

Individual faculty persons are interested in and receptive to tackling new and important problems, but they are reluctant to have to fight their home department and all the academic bureaucracy to do it. One of the challenges of administration must be to make this conflict minimal. One student of a university organization called for strategy of planned flexibility which can gain flexibility without destroying the positive contributions and security provided by department and college structures. The program director approach is an attempt to do just this.

The mechanics and details of approaches will differ among institutions, and they should. But the key to progress remains the same—leadership must take the position that rural community development is a problem. It is a mission area that is important to the agricultural complex; we belong in the area with our teaching, research, and extension activities, and we should devote resources to it.

Some people want no change to upset their domain, but this does not seem to be a widespread condition of our faculties. Many faculty members—perhaps the majority—can and want to participate in new directions and new activities. The challenge is to capitalize on and utilize this latter group and not be immobilized in our thoughts and actions by the former group.

If we recognize this mission as an important one and facilitate good people to give it attention, good and useful research will result.

We should not be hindered by the possibility that all the necessary talent may not reside within agriculture on our various campuses. We should move creatively with what we have; cooperation with other disciplines will be forthcoming when we become a growing concern with purpose and direction. On the opposite side of the coin, we should not be overenthused about diverting our resources into other areas of the university without some specific prearrangements. One unique dimension of agriculture is its mission orientation and the protection of this mission through the experiment station and the cooperative extension service. This type of dedication and organization is not widely duplicated throughout the total campus. If we are to receive further resources for pursuing this area, we will be held accountable for their use. It becomes especially important that our concern now be focused on the farmer, his community, and the total well-being of rural America.

We certainly cannot await the complete consensus of everyone concerning the importance of the problem, its dimensions, and its orientation before we move. To await such consensus in any new or innovative area is a major way to stifle change.

CHAPTER ELEVEN

NEW PRIORITIES

EARL O. HEADY

RURAL AMERICA is in the process of undevelopment—retreating relatively and absolutely in labor force, population, capital inflow, commerce, community structure, and income generation from its pinnacle of a half-century ago. Behind the tides of undevelopment is a set of powerful forces or variables. These forces are created through relative prices for capital and labor; through the biological and mechanical improvements generated by our public land-grant colleges and the private sector; through the stage and spatial configuration of economic development in a wealthy country which emphasizes services and other products of human capital and migration to urban or growth centers accordingly; and through changing consumer preferences, cultural orientations, and life styles that draw people to larger population centers. These are extremely strong forces. The few research workers concerned with the structure of agriculture and rural communities (plus a few educational experts) are faced with not one giant but (a) thousands of them producing new technologies that substitute capital for labor and land in agriculture and (b) millions of them reshaping consumer patterns to the products and life styles that are apart from those supplied in small rural settlements.

The problems involved in stemming or diverting this tide are complex and tremendous. They require many more people in research, education, and advisory capacities. The number of research workers now engaged in these activities cannot possibly meet the expectations of the public and university administrators. The manpower is simply too sparse, both in this region and nationally.

EARL O. HEADY is Charles F. Curtiss Distinguished Professor of Agriculture; Professor of Economics; Director, North Central Regional Center for Rural Development; Director, Center for Agricultural and Rural Development, Iowa State University.

CHALLENGES AND OPPORTUNITIES. While the problems are
complex and the task is tremendous relative to the manpower currently available, they present both a challenge and an opportunity for the land-grant universities. These public institutions were
created as the "people's colleges." The training of students was one
designated purpose, but their creators also set forth for them the task
of solving people's problems in practical ways. In the early days it
was not difficult to find the relevant people and problems. These colleges basically were located (most of them still are) in rural states and
rural areas of all states. Their major clientele and problems were
clearly those of farmers. Because further technical improvement and
supply capacity meshed with demand conditions of the time, drawing
both more labor and capital into agriculture, they also served the
nonfarm rural people in an indirect but very real and commercial
manner. The greater income and inflow of consumer and producer
goods had a multiplier effect that may have brought even greater
benefits to the rural merchants and public employees. The "people's
colleges" put little effort into appealing to the nonfarm population
of rural areas; now they must put forth more effort or lose their rural
clientele completely.

We are in a technical position and economic environment where
each biological advance and mechanical innovation generated in the
agricultural colleges is quickly translated into a reduction in the farm
labor force and the number of farms. Augmented by parallel efforts
of private industry, the traditional and ongoing thrust of the agricultural colleges is hurrying the day when the number of farms to be
served by them will dwindle to 150,000 nationally and about 3,000
per state. This is certainly the direction and result when, as now, the
agricultural colleges of the region (or even nation) have only a few
dozen research workers to treat the problems of economic and social
structure of rural communities but thousands of researchers whose
efforts are rapidly translated into fewer people in rural communities
and many fewer but much larger farms. Under the demand elastici-
ties of the times and national policies to restrain supplies to a given
level, each set of biological innovations that increases the corn yield
by five bushels per acre substitutes equivalently for 20,000 farm
workers. And the effects of today's physical and mechanical marvels
are equal or greater in impact on the rural community.

The current mix of research programs in agricultural colleges is
one in which the impact of results that cause reductions in the farm
work force, number of farms, and employment opportunities of rural
towns dwarfs the power of results from research designed to resolve
income, welfare, population, and equity problems of rural communities. Few public universities in the region can appeal for support in
exchange for help so effectively as through the problems of rural community development or welfare. But none has yet put forth a major

appeal for finances in terms of the urgency, complexity, and breadth of rural community problems—even though these are the dominant problems of the majority of states in the region. No land-grant university has put rural development as the major item on its agenda of affairs presented to the state. In the rural communities where the majority of nonmetropolitan populations reside and rest their economic dependence, local economies are in a rapid state of decline. The number of farmers is dwindling rapidly, and the occupants of the villages and small towns have growing problems and reduced welfare accordingly. Aside from serving as a vehicle for human capital investment for the benefit of youth in enhanced earning power, the major benefit that universities in most states of our region can supply is in treatment of the problems of rural areas. Here is an opportunity for our universities to acquire a much greater and more vigorous clientele than at the present. Here is an opportunity for them to appeal for more resources and get a favorable hearing. While they will be asking for more funds when the next legislative sessions roll around, probably no land-grant university will present a major program in rural development to be funded. There will be requests for more research funds, but along such conventional avenues as more chemistry research with potential use by and employment in urban factories and more plant research to increase cereal yields to be later offset by greater public expenditure on farm supply control programs.

The mistake for the land-grant universities, especially the agricultural colleges and experiment stations, is less in requesting funds of general scientific nature and more in failure to ask for funds to mount the research needed for the massive problems of rural areas. The agricultural colleges and experiment stations must turn in this direction if they are not to work themselves out of a job. They may claim that they have such programs, but the manpower so devoted is very small compared to the personnel in those fields that generate the new technology causing farms and rural towns to vanish.

The opportunity is there for those institutions that truly want to extend their clientele and services to the total citizenry and problem set of rural communities—in other than a superficial manner and with more than lip-service to the commitment. Resources can be made available to those institutions that present an earnest and well-packaged prospectus of the problems and a serious promise of contributing to their solutions. The audience then to be served is much broader and larger than under the traditional, and still ongoing, overwhelming focus on the largest and most commercial of farms. Will the agricultural colleges and experiment stations meet this challenge? Or will they let it pass by, therein setting the stage for their own diminished role and support for the future? From the standpoint of both federal and state funds, the agricultural colleges and experiment stations are at the crossroads. They can maintain their main focus on the technical and organizational aspects of the most commercial farms, with minute attention to the broader problems around them in rural communities, and remain on a plateau in funds (and thus a declining portion of total research funds); or they can come to grips with the major economic and social problems that prevail over most of the space of our states (those of rural communities), make themselves heard and understood, and claim broader funds and publics accordingly.

Agricultural colleges and experiment stations must maintain strong programs in technology and organization of commercial farms for several reasons: (1) as a guarantee against uncertainty and contingencies surrounding long-run world control of population, food supplies, and the environment; (2) the competitive position of the United States in world markets and in leadership ability to provide aid in world food and developmental problems; (3) because, even though demand for food is elastic, policies are possible that allow gains (a) to consumers in lower real prices for food as resource requirements decline and simultaneously (b) to farm producers if supply is controlled and managed appropriately. The means for this positive-sum outcome from technical change between large commercial farmers and consumers-at-large has been fairly well implemented over the last two decades and is a worthy accomplishment (even if there may be more efficient and less costly means to attain exactly the same goal). But a positive-sum outcome overall is not guaranteed if we allow the burden of technical change to fall on small farms, the business sector, and a disproportionate number of low-income persons in rural areas. As a minimum compensation, rural communities are owed as much research, planning, and guiding effort as goes into research that changes the structure and reduces the number of farms, bringing on the economic and social problems of rural communities.

DEVELOPMENT AND RESEARCH ALLOCATIONS. The very processes of farm and national development that give rise to the economic, welfare, and equity problems of rural communities also provide a rather large and logical set of funds for pursuing research on these specific problems. At low stages of development, as at the initiation of land-grant universities, the major inputs of agriculture are land and labor. Under this input mix with a small market for capital items, the main technical improvements must come from publicly financed research. Private firms have few opportunities for fabrication and sale of capital items; hence they conduct little research. But as development occurs and the inputs of the farming sector become mainly capital items (as they are now in the North

Central Region and the United States), the market for capital items becomes large. An individual private firm can enhance its competitive position and enlarge the demand for its capital products if it conducts research to make them more productive and discovers innovations of low real price. This trend is reflected in the fact that private research expenditures for agriculture now exceed those of public institutions. Hence a certain set of public funds is thus released for research on problems caused by technological progress in agriculture, especially on problems of rural areas. Since the private sector will fill in and carry the one phase of research—that related to testing and immediate yield increases—the public institutions will have both a logical and rather large source of funds to be diverted to rural area research. We have not gone far in these shifts which would appeal to the large publics of rural communities and more nearly guarantee the agricultural experiment stations and the technical disciplines a source of funding for the future. The possibilities of reapplications of research resources apply not only to the social sciences; many fields of engineering and physical sciences can have an important role in replanning, guiding, and restructuring rural communities. Some personnel from the latter fields would certainly find this research more exciting than the traditional orientations to which institutions and customs now hold them.

The acquisition and reallocation of research funds and personnel can provide the land-grant colleges an opportunity to show their publics that they still exist to serve them—especially in those states where the major problems are those of rural communities (as in the North Central Region). But for some time, research workers concerned with economic and social systems of rural communities and their interrelationships with larger regional systems will probably be faced with funds that are extremely scarce relative to the magnitude and complexity of the problems facing them. Consequently, some careful calculation must be applied to determine which problems should be attacked first. The resources are far too few to allow us to do research on the problems each community wishes us to do. In this setting of large and complex problems and very few resources, the payoff will likely be greatest in two general areas—namely, public policies and group solutions that prevail or apply generally across many or all communities faced with problems of inadequate or declining income, employment, welfare, and social and environmental services. If restitution in equity and opportunity is provided relevant communities, there is not much time to become highly involved in research mechanics of interest and utility mainly to the scientific community. The most relevant communities and population strata are not the towns that "have everything going for them" in added industry and employment opportunity but those that inequitably bear the major costs of selective economic and population shifts. They are the groups and communities with reduced or restrained income and employment opportunities, an increasing proportion of aged, declining or inadequate medical and health services, large relative costs of public services, depressing social environments, and decreasing recreational opportunities.

OUR OWN PRIORITIES. To make our resources most productive in terms of persons reached and helped, we must concentrate on those who have been bearing the costs (or are so threatened) of economic development and reorganization, especially that stemming from the technological transformation of agriculture. For example, a state might select its endowment of natural resources as an opportunity for development to draw other persons into the community for recreational purposes. Yet those who have effective demand for boating, camping, and hunting typically are middle-class and rather high income families who have opportunities for recreation in other directions. Is this project as important as one that deals with recreational opportunities and social environment for older persons in a purely small-town farm community that has neither an endowment of natural resources to be developed or any positive mechanism for recreation and social interaction among this lower-income and immobile population stratum?

Policies, systems, and groups that are common to or prevail over many communities are emphasized because scarce research funds can be best made to go further for the relevant problem set. Also, some problems can be best "lifted out" for manageable, independent study in this manner. For example, the relative emphasis of policies that concentrate on the poor and rich of cities and on rich farmers in all rural communities have a universal application in the sense that they neglect generally the relative concentration of low-income, underemployed, and disadvantaged persons in rural areas. The paucity, nature, and potentials of health service supply also compose a problem subset common to a vast number of rural communities. Welfare and public service systems and costs and the milieu surrounding aged populations represent problems that extend over the majority of communities. Regional economic systems that embrace a large number of community economic systems, which also can be related to larger urban-oriented or national economic systems, also pose research endeavors and policy possibilities that can simultaneously embrace a number of communities.

Not all studies that treat the individual community as an entity should be ignored. There are studies of decision processes, for example, that could have application to many other communities functioning under parallel conditions of natural endowment, developmental decay, and economic environment. Studies that indicate optimal structural reorganizations for communities (the majority) which have no great industrialization prospects and must adapt to smaller populations, fewer farms, and even fewer towns and villages would fall in a similar category.

We are pressed for answers today of yesterday's problems. This condition of urgency has arisen partly because those who obtain and administer research funds in our universities and governments paid little heed to those who documented and detailed the upcoming nature and urgency of the problems. Now these problems are coming to the fore and being popularized by politicians who desire election, by government administrators long following the wrong path to solve the wrong problem, by city leaders looking to population dispersion to solve urban ills, and by the growing awareness and pressure of rural citizens who are not major recipients of subsidies to large commercial farms. While these pressures for instant answers and research prevail, some base in fundamental research and quantification of relevant basic models must be accomplished. The problem set will not vanish soon; in parts of many states it will grow more severe in the next decade. To provide more and better answers for the questions of five to ten years from now, some base needs to be laid in fundamental models and research directed toward eventual empirical choices and solutions.

EQUITY EMPHASIS. High priority must be given to the problems of those persons, groups, and communities that sacrifice most as a result of our ongoing farm technological transformation and the spatial and demographic impacts of national economic growth. Both of these sets of forces concentrate problems of inequity in rural communities. The challenging task in rural community development is to identify the nature, location, and extent of inequities falling on rural communities and various population strata of them and then to evaluate and provide alternative means for alleviating or redressing them. A central challenge is to eliminate the inequities in low income, underemployment, and unfavorable living and welfare conditions in nonmetropolitan areas. In a few favored locations an important extent of these inequities can be erased through industrialization. In a greater number, however, the inequities can be removed only through entirely different means and programs. Elimination of inequities or provision of economic and social opportunity must be through public means and policies.

Inequitable distribution of the gains and sacrifices of development among communities and between metropolitan and nonmetropolitan areas now promises to be the foundation upon which broader public concerns over rural development will be built. Twenty years ago the primary national concern was growth without regard to its spatial distribution or the distribution of its social and economic costs and benefits. Growth in GNP was given nearly the entire weight in the national objective function, just as it still is in many developing countries. Zero weight was given the variables of decline in rural or spatially and market-isolated communities. It has been less than a decade since many spokesmen championed growth in aggregate GNP as the sole major solution of farm and rural area problems, some even measuring the magnitude of growth in GNP required to absorb the flow of labor from agriculture and rural communities. But just as unrestrained and aggregate growth at the national level spawns a complex distribution of costs and benefits among regions and communities, a single goal of development at state levels also can bring inequitable distribution between metropolitan and nonmetropolitan areas or among rural communities. If development is sought without regard to its distribution effects, the programs and processes have a single dimension. The "name of the game" is almost entirely industrialization (or an equivalent such as recreational development or tourism). We would be adding industries where they have the most obvious advantage and where the thrust typically is already in this direction because of endowments such as natural resources, location, existing transportation networks, and large public installations. We would be neglecting all other communities that are in the process of decline. To those who have gains, we would bring more; to those experiencing social and economic costs, we would add to the burden.

INDEX